SUSI|

Transform
to
Outperform

7 powers to transform you,
your team and your results

First published in Great Britain by Practical Inspiration Publishing, 2022

© Susie Robinson, 2022

The moral rights of the author have been asserted

ISBN   9781788603737   (print)
           9781788603751   (epub)
           9781788603744   (mobi)

Every effort has been made to trace copyright holders and to obtain their permission for the use of copyright material. The publisher apologizes for any errors or omissions and would be grateful if notified of any corrections that should be incorporated in future reprints or editions of this book.

Want to bulk-buy copies of this book for your team and colleagues? We can introduce case studies, customize the content and co-brand *Transform to Outperform* to suit your business's needs.

Please email info@practicalinspiration.com for more details.

Practical Inspiration
Publishing

Contents

Introduction

'Transformation' is arguably the buzzword of the decade; it seems there's a business or digital transformation story in every news feed. There's no getting away from it – transformation is the new stability. Whether comfortable, frustrated, or at the top of our game, we must transform to stay relevant, to prevent decline, or defend against disruptive forces. If staying relevant or defending disruption doesn't motivate you, perhaps the idea of outperformance grabs your attention. Maybe you want to do better than you have done so far, or you want to beat the performance of your peers and competitors. You are in the right place.

You may be wondering whether transformation is old wine in new bottles. After all, change and change management aren't new. Well, at some level they are the same. Change implies something finite and granular, which is substituted for something else. Transform, on the other hand, infers a significant evolution or metamorphosis from one state to another, where the foundation remains intact, yet in a new guise; it looks, feels, and performs radically better than before. Following a personal transformation for example, the core personality, skills, and physical person are the same; however, the person may look, feel, behave, and perform considerably better. Change management is a group of practices for helping people and organizations achieve change; tools to be used during transformation.

During my 35-year career in the field of human resources and people development, I was privileged to work at a top executive level in a successful global business, interfacing with other leading organizations across geographies and industry sectors. Transformation became an enduring feature of my work, the inevitable side effect of business transfers, international mergers and acquisitions, technology, and a perpetual dissatisfaction with the status quo. I led the people and culture transformations arising out of global mergers and business functions. I learned the hard way what works and doesn't. It is this experience of complexity and challenge, of failure and success, which compels me to share my ideas to help or inspire others.

This book is intended for leaders seeking to transform their own results and those of their team and organization. It also offers human resources professionals a tool to help business partners do the same. Inside, I outline the seven powers required to transform and outperform, which, when activated, make you and your team difficult to beat: Personal Power, Goal Power, Process Power, People Power, Culture Power, Smart Power, and Staying Power. I have sought to provide practical help and tools where possible, and occasional insights into culture, psychology, neuroscience, and performance science, where they matter.

A leader's role is all about transformation, whether of the team's performance or the business results, and it always begins at home; to transform others and their results, we must first unlock our own power and superpower. To bring this idea home, I have decrypted the stories of some well-known transformation super-heroes and their outstanding performance. The term 'superpower' is a trendy cliche, typically used to describe strengths; by the end of the book, you will understand how and when strengths *truly* become superpowers. The application of the seven powers in the book are described in the context of transforming an organization, however, it does not require a great leap of imagination to see their relevance in any situation. I promise that if you apply what you learn here, adjusted to your context, you will experience greater personal success and pride as you watch your team outperform.

In Chapter 1, we explore the case for transformation, get under the hood of what it means to outperform, and meet our first trans-formation superhero. Chapter 2 is based on my personal experi-ence of releasing personal power, through discovery of strengths, personality, and values; how to take responsibility for your story;

and how to release your very own superpower. In Chapter 3, the focus is on building a purpose for your team, a compelling vision, goals, a plan, setting up the conditions for making it happen, and creating momentum. Chapter 4 offers tools for leading and digesting change within the organization. Specifically, we explore the reactions to change, the toxic behaviours that arise and how to respond. In Chapter 5, people power includes the sourcing, engagement, and development of your supporting team and the creation of an environment for high performance, wellbeing, and positive mental health. We go on to decode four cultural themes for high performance in Chapter 6: what it takes to create an extraordinary employee experience in a people culture; how to use constructive accountability and consequences to create an accountable culture; how to achieve the personalization and the intimacy edge of a customer culture; and how to embody the irresistible quality of a culture of excellence. In Chapter 7, we explore the sources of power and influence in organizations and focus on the use of smart and mainly soft power as the means to sustain transformation. Chapter 8 outlines the essence of staying power, the resilience required to stay the course. Finally, the conclusion provides a summary of an outperforming organization, team, and leader. Inevitably in a book about leaders, people, and cultures, some topics appear more than once; coaching, culture, and teamworking, for example. I have avoided repetition by adding only new information and including cross-references where appropriate.

Devour these chapters and in doing so you are a step closer to outperformance. For the complete chronological outline, read the whole text or, if you prefer, flick between chapters to focus on areas of interest. All case studies are blended, adjusted, or fictionalized for anonymity and effect. Each chapter concludes with a list of action points to help the reader convert key learnings into practical steps. This book is neither an academic work nor a prescription; it's a guide based on practical experience and reflections on my own experiments in life, informed as far as possible by experts in their field, some of whom I have worked with personally. Whether or not you agree with the ideas presented, I hope more than anything you discover inspiration and help me fulfil my ambition to activate game-changing outperformance in others.

Chapter 1

Transform to outperform

Introduction

Transformation occurs continuously and often invisibly, below the surface of our lives. In this chapter, we bring into focus the features of a successful transformation journey, the triggers and counterintuitive moments that indicate a need to transform, and the perils of ignoring these signals. We go on to distinguish characteristics of organizational outperformance and to introduce the seven powers that enable team and individual outperformance.

Transform

As natural as breathing.

During a recent fitness drive I was reminded of the human capacity for transformation. Not, I assure you, as a result of my reflection in the mirror but because I am fascinated with the idea of intermittent fasting to stimulate ketosis, a process during which the body breaks down fat stores for energy when starved of food or carbohydrates, and autophagy (meaning eating oneself), which occurs after prolonged fasting. Cells recycle and regenerate, disposing of waste and damaged proteins, and the waste product supplies fuel for energy, a process which allows the body's tissues and cells to renew completely. Amazing, don't you think? Transformation is as natural as breathing; we are creatures of constant regeneration when we create the right conditions. If we can renew and improve our body when we treat it right, surely we can renew and improve our behaviours, personalities, and our results.

Life is a perpetual reinvention made up of experiences and formative moments, a performance in which we are the star, with

1

highs, lows and a supporting cast. If we take a moment to explore our past we can see how far we've come. Perhaps you recall delighting your parents with new skills as a child, how a teacher spotted your potential, a first job, a significant experience, a new connection; these events and interactions, often the result of chance, transformed you and your outcomes. Imagine what you could achieve if you were *really* trying. Mohandas Gandhi said, 'If we could change ourselves, the tendencies in the world would also change. As a man changes his own nature, so does the attitude of the world change towards him'. It's so true; the more we transform with purpose, vision, and discipline, the greater our influence and ability to achieve great things. When we plan our career and life moments for their transformation potential, we become better versions of ourselves, produce new results, and experience an improved reality. From my vantage point in international human resources, I have seen how leadership is about transforming outcomes. It begins with dissatisfaction, a focus on something that needs to change. Soon enough, we realize we must transform ourselves and the team to make it happen. With passion, strengths, a commitment to transform into our best self, and a corresponding plan for the team and the business, we generate peak performance.

The transformation journey

Transformation is always more difficult than it appears. Who hasn't attempted a body transformation at some time? Instinctively we know the problem has something to do with eating less and exercising more. If it's so obvious, why is there an enormous gap between knowing what to do and doing it? It's because hidden influences of the mind, body, culture, and lifestyle create a more complex problem than we realize. Those who manage to achieve and sustain the change over time know the recipe:

❖ A deep understanding of the problem and a sense of what must happen for change to be achieved.

❖ A purpose and motivation to act. A genuine desire to improve born out of dissatisfaction.

❖ Sacrifice of something important. Removal of barriers or reasons that have until now maintained the status quo.

❖ A vision or target outcome, a lucid image of success.

❖ A plan to turn the vision into manageable steps from start to finish.

❖ Milestone goals and measurement. A plan, and goals to create action and chart progress.

❖ A process, a pragmatic and actionable method. A personalized regime with rules and a routine.

❖ Daily intentions. Flexible mini steps towards a bigger goal.

❖ A supporting team. Colleagues, friends, and family who assist, hold us to account, and provide advice and motivational support.

❖ Modification of habits, behaviours, and activities. Transformed actions and behaviours, the small elements of routine which replace bad or inefficient habits.

❖ Discipline and focus. A personal commitment, the self-control and ability to stay on course. A new culture.

Whether it's a desire to lose weight, change team performance, or reconstruct an organization, the recipe is the same. Transformation is about people; whatever the practice to be transformed, it only happens when people change how they interact with it.

Call to action

Why does 'Transform to outperform' resonate? Are you keen to improve your team's performance or do you just want to get ahead? Perhaps you're feeling lost, missing a purpose, or disconnected?

Discomfort is an emotional state, often stimulated by outside influences, and characterized by negative emotions like anger, confusion, fear, or pain. These visceral responses are survival instincts designed to make us act; they tell us it's time to do something different. In August 2005 Senator Barack Obama was busy writing his book *The Audacity of Hope*. His wife Michelle, in her book *Becoming*, says 'He really was content, he told me, to stay where he was, building his influence over time.'[1] He flew to Houston and spent time with evacuees of the Hurricane Katrina disaster in New Orleans; meeting these people and witnessing the tragedy firsthand inspired a transformation and the run for the US Presidency. 'The experience kindled something in him, that nagging sense he wasn't yet doing enough', Michelle concludes. Not every transformation has such a dramatic cause or effect, but they do create important progress. A process may feel outdated, other teams perform better, business growth or profits are diminished, costs are too high, customer satisfaction levels low, or the business is lagging the competition and in need of technological innovation. When individuals or organizations experience the nagging feeling of discomfort, it is time to change. Procrastination ends in crisis when a problem becomes too big to ignore.

Throughout history, *disruption* has occurred with the advent of major inventions which transform everyday life: the telephone, the car, the printing press, the airplane, for example. The evolution that followed innovations was slow at first, momentum built, ideas gained popularity, and the world adapted. The web and other technological innovations disrupt on a daily basis. Established businesses find their model upended by unconventional new entrants, operating quietly on the fringes of their market. A radical inflection point occurs, and the unanticipated or underestimated competitor redefines value, surges, and captures the market. Notable examples include large and respected companies like Nokia with mobile

---

[1]   Michelle Obama, *Becoming*, Penguin Random House, 2018, p. 220.

phones and RIM with the Blackberry, whose market-leading position dissipated overnight when the smart phone landed. Even giants like Sony, the leader in consumer electronics with their focus on high-quality products and innovation, were caught short. Sony failed to understand the impact of digital and were ambushed by Apple products which stormed their apparent safe market position. The iPod's ability to store thousands of music tracks and iTunes' facilitation of pay per track crushed the CD market. The iPhone and iPad with high-quality images and videos displaced cameras and quickly became the technology of choice. Early detection of disruptive influences requires intense market scanning, obsessive customer trend analysis, constant testing of innovation, the ability to respond decisively, and the courage to embark on the upheaval of change.

When we slip into routines and feel we have achieved the results of our efforts, we feel comfortable. It's where we get time to consolidate learning and achieve balance, a time to relax perhaps? Unfortunately, not. *Comfort* leads to apathy and complacency. Being comfortable is a signal that we are at our peak, potentially heading for decline. When business is booming and the team performing, we should be immersed in a plan to change course. It's time to deploy the tools of storm prediction so that resources can be redirected. If we only act in the eye of the storm, we are consumed with fighting the problem; the emergency sucks in energy, financial and human resources, limiting opportunity to invest in a progressive solution. For example, nations and businesses anticipated a pandemic for years; they designed pandemic response solutions, wrote emergency business continuity plans, and conducted simulations. Scientists and experts warned of transmission risks and potential courses of action, yet most countries failed to act until COVID-19 had taken hold. Comfort and complacency devastated lives.

A new S curve

Some years ago, when persuading reluctant leaders to transform practices in a manufacturing company, I helpfully stumbled upon the work of Charles Handy in *The Age of the Paradox*. Handy's management theory is underpinned by the mathematical concept of the sigmoid curve, an S-shaped curve which represents the natural life cycle of all things (life, business, career etc.). The curve depicts a dip at the start, a steep rise, followed by a peak and a decline to the end. Consider the performance of a team: the initial dip in the curve represents a period of forming, experimenting, and learning. When the team become established, the curve inclines as performance increases. Peak performance is achieved and sustained until the context or environment change, causing decline, unless a timely decision is made to transform.

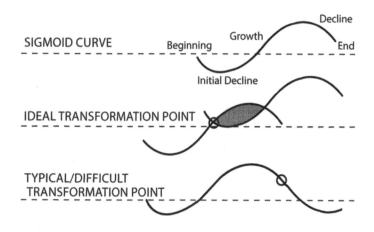

Figure 1: Sigmoid curve of transformation[2]

---

[2] Image adapted from Rosemary Hipkins and Bronwen Cowie, 'The sigmoid curve as a metaphor for growth and change', *Teachers and Curriculum*, 2016;16(2). Available from https://files.eric.ed.gov/fulltext/EJ1123357.pdf [accessed 19 May 2022].

A new curve must begin whilst the first one can still support it. Success is likely when transformation is initiated before the first curve peaks, whilst still on the rise, since resources, energy, and confidence are high. Plans fail when we wait too long and attempt to transform in a state of decline and reduced capability, as indicated in the following case study.

Transforming after the peak

ABC company grew and transformed successfully by adjusting market position and acquiring new capabilities. During a global downturn, however, declining profits and the loss of a key account blindsided the leadership. The slump exposed operational weaknesses, up until now veiled by impressive-looking operations and strong profits. The executive team sought help and set a course for bold transformation and ambitious growth. Project teams overhauled business development and delivery. A newly hired sales force deployed an improved commercial process. Communications intensified, and employees rallied around a brand name for the change. The organization began to see the benefits of the growth strategy. Programme management was strong, review processes effective, and progress routinely chalked up, creating an air of optimism. Operating divisions, however, continued to experience challenges and simultaneously began to feel the pains of change. Damaging operational losses and financial pitfalls in the sales process appeared, creating panic in the top team. In crisis, they halted the transformation and turned to containment. The scale of performance issues, fiscal challenge, and a substantial new business pipeline caused a 'pipe burst'. The leadership were not committed to their vision for the future. They abandoned the investment, salvaging only those features which could support the organization in improving the cash position and operational performance.

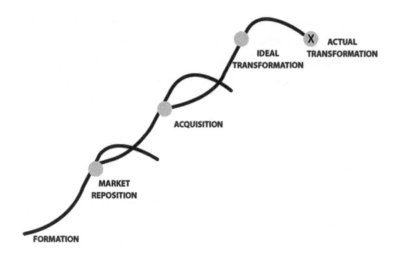

Figure 2: ABC company growth

To avoid a similar fate, we must live with the idea that our business is always unfinished, a sense that systems, processes, or practice always need improvement. As one goal is fulfilled, another more challenging one sits on the horizon. Whilst processes embed, diagnosis of the next transformation begins. This constant state of anticipation is overwhelming and stressful; our natural urge is to slip into routine, reliability, and comfort. Leaders can increase the sense of stability and completion for employees and clients by illustrating a bridge between old and new ways of working, helping them see new process as a logical evolution, providing continuity, consistency of vision, good communication, and clear course charting.

In the case of ABC company, it was easy to get lost in the euphoria of growth and comfortable profits. The top team delayed action in favour of channelling resources towards urgent operational issues. Timely action would have inflicted profit reductions against key accounts, a medicine too unsavoury to take. A state of denial crept into the leadership subconscious. Once the decline began, the company were forced into a destructive cycle of cost cutting and firefighting. Had the leadership remedied performance deficiencies and addressed commercial issues with customers during the good times, had they invested in new skills and reinvented critical processes ahead of the peak, they would have initiated a new curve. Disruptive influence or discomfort which gnaw in the gut require attention. When an operational or commercial weakness is worrying and no one is talking about it, heed the warning and surface issues for discussion. Address the problem; don't wait until it requires disproportionate effort and resources.

Disruption signals

Disruptive inflection points begin with weak signals around the edges. They are difficult to interpret, and threats seem insignificant. Amazon, for example, was initially perceived as an online bookstore. This giant global e-commerce, cloud computing, digital streaming, and artificial intelligence company is one of a handful of global technology companies changing the world and disrupting industries, supply chains, and households. Amazon's early activities did not reveal clear data signals and warnings; their impact was not fully understood or addressed strategically by competitors. Amazon has fundamentally altered the basis of competition in the industries in which it participates. It provides an irresistible competitive advantage, smashes through entry barriers, and can provide value to customers all over the world. The rise of Amazon and similar online merchants is decimating the traditional retail business model, leaving many high streets in decline. In a 1999 recorded interview with Jeff Bezos, founder of Amazon, he discusses his vision of obsessive customer service, enabled by large distribution facilities, the internet, and information to support customer purchasing decisions. The interviewer challenges the complexity and cost, but Bezos argues that the cost of distribution real estate fades in comparison to that of setting up networks of premium-sited retail stores.[3] The clues were there for the taking.

---

[3] Jeff Bezos, CNBC interview, 1999. Available from https://m.youtube.com/watch?v=GltlJO56S1g [accessed 19 May 2022].

Retailers could have used their dominance and financial fire power to transform in a way that would mitigate the effect of Amazon and other online merchants. Most large retailers set up multi-channel services and an internet presence; however, they are still funding flagship high street stores as well as distribution centres and finding it difficult to survive. Where were the top consultants with their intelligence and analytics, urging the retail industry to transform? The Amazon story conveys a message to business and teams: standing still is not an option. Everything ends and when it does it's either irrelevant, undesirable, adds no value, outdated, or dead! If the team and company performance seem impossible to beat, it's a signal to divert attention and resources to a new vision. The inevitable decline will happen, at which time it may be too late, too expensive, or too difficult to transform.

Consider your current position. Do you feel discomfort about the performance of the team, their processes, or practices? Are you worried about remote trends? Are things too good now? What are the looming macro-economic factors and uncertainties? Are you working on big data, analytics, and artificial intelligence with your team? Trust your instincts and explore options for action. The process takes time, and the details depend upon whether the transformation affects you, your team, your organization, even your industry. The key to outperformance is you; your ability to unleash personal power, lead, inspire, and coach the transformation of your team and their results. We will therefore explore personal power in Chapter 2.

Outperform

To do or perform better than someone or something.

We possess an intrinsic drive to move forward rather than stand still and are drawn towards being part of something great; we relish moments of exceptional performance when we alone, or our team or company, exceed expectations or achieve something better than the rest. It's what makes work and life matter. Let's consider, therefore, what it means to outperform.

Organizational outperformance

Business performance is measured using financial ratios, profit and loss, year-on-year growth, share price, and other indicators. To determine outperformance, results must be compared with industry competitors over time. In Jim Collins' classic book *Good to Great*,[4] the companies deemed great were those that outperformed their industry over a sustained period. Performance was measured by assessing the ratio of cumulative stock returns compared with their industry. The nominated companies reached a transition point in their development when results jumped from good to great, which they maintained for at least 15 years. This work revealed seven concepts as enablers of organizational outperformance: In the process of becoming good, these companies are led by **Level 5 leaders** who are ambitious for the company and demonstrate humility and professional will. They are understated, diligent, and fanatical about achieving results, whatever it takes; they are rigorous, not ruthless in people decisions, and avoid toxic layoff strategies to obtain profit improvements. Amazon's Jeff Bezos is a level 5 leader. He is famous now, yet did not court hero worship, nor demand slavish allegiance; he quietly and fiercely pursued his passion. **First who… then what**. Good companies are rigorous about people selection before strategy, vision, or anything else. The right team become part of the vision and strategy, as wedded to it as the leader, so that they can continue when the leader moves on. Leaders of good companies **confront brutal facts** and maintain confidence in success, despite adversity. In an established

---

[4] Jim Collins, *Good to Great: Why Some Companies Make the Leap and Others Don't*, Random House Business Books, 2001, pp. 6–8, 35–38, 47, 89, 90, 101, 119, 120–153, 175.

business this might mean taking decisions such as exiting a successful product line. For Amazon it was the courage to sustain and defend investment whilst unprofitable, with certain faith that results would come.

The transition from good, and the steep rise to greatness occur when complexity is simplified into a single organizing idea, a **hedgehog concept** that guides everything; the name originates from a Greek parable which states 'The fox knows many things, but the hedgehog knows one big thing'. In the story, the fox tries to catch the hedgehog but is always outsmarted by the hedgehog who does one thing very well: defending itself by rolling into a spiky ball. It takes about four years for a company to get to this stage. Such companies debate and experiment to gain deep understanding of the answer to three questions. First, what are we deeply passionate about? Second, what can we be best in the world at? The company may have a competence but not the capacity to be best in the world, or they may have the capacity to be the best in the world at something for which they do not hold the current competence. Amazon's Jeff Bezos pursued a big hairy audacious goal to be 'The Everything Store'. Third, what drives our economic engine? What is the single economic denominator that has the biggest impact? Profit per x or cash flow per x.

Sustained results and greatness are built on a **culture of self-disciplined people** who think and act in a disciplined way, consistent with their 'hedgehog concept'. Great companies and their disciplined people are not tempted to deviate from their single idea by the prize of 'one-off' attractions. They use resources on activities that fit closest with their single idea and are uncompromising in the way they measure themselves against their original goals. They are also selective about technology which must fit their unifying concept and accelerate momentum rather than create it – **technology accelerators**. Finally, these endeavours combine until one day there is a **flywheel effect**. The compound effect of one action on the other causes the virtual flywheel to turn. Without additional effort, every small step puts pressure on the flywheel, increases momentum, and generates breakthrough results. Amazon's flywheel begins with an obsessive customer experience which drives traffic, which in turn attracts sellers and provides customers with more choice. Sales increase, allowing costs and prices to be reduced, which enables a better customer experience which drives traffic. This powerful flywheel is a contributor to the downfall of many complacent organizations, sitting in Amazon's backdraught.[5]

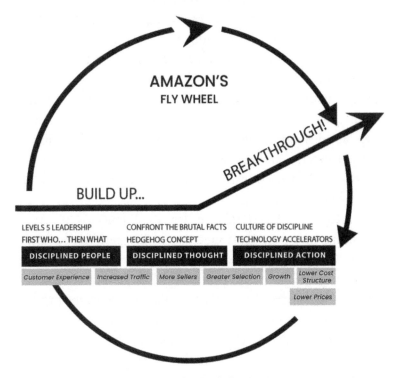

Figure 3: Amazon's flywheel[6]

[5] Lance Peppler, 'The amazing Flywheel Effect – succeed like Amazon', *The Business Bookshelf*, 18 October 2019. Available from www.businessbookshelfpodcast.com/post/the-amazing-flywheel-effect-succeed-like-amazon [accessed 19 May 2022].
[6] Image redrawn and adapted from Jim Collins, *Good to Great*, Random House Business Books, 2001, p. 12.

Team and individual outperformance

An organization's results are the combined result of high-performing individuals, leaders, and teams doing the right things. Business leaders and teams are typically rewarded against performance measures of their operating unit; if targets and budgets are determined effectively, the operating unit measure is a good indication of team success. These outcomes can be compared with other teams to determine whether one team performs better than another over time. Measuring individual performance, however, is trickier because of the interconnected nature of the team's activities. A leader affects results through decisions, whilst team member contributions may not be as distinct. To address this challenge, organizations turn to descriptors of competence, against which observable behaviours and outcomes are compared. Judgements are still subjective and human resource teams must arbitrate and calibrate to defend against the bias of managers who over- or underrate their team.

During annual performance debates, I routinely observed how teams whose business unit topped the performance table were happy enough; results were considered a reflection of the leader and the team. When results were off target, business leaders fought to demonstrate 'one-off' events that hampered their ability to achieve results, and for which the team deserved consideration. Underperforming teams also complained that higher performers profited from soft targets, whilst they themselves suffered from unrealistic targets. An illustration of the frailty and subjectivity of human performance measures.

Difficult as performance measurement can be, it is necessary. Goals are signposts that tell us we are on the right track. Comparison with these goals and the performance of others is how we know we are achieving our potential. Goal power, explored in Chapter 3, is one of seven enabling powers of individual, leader, and team performance which are mapped onto the flywheel below. Performance begins with the release of personal power, which is activated and amplified by goal and process power. Individuals can also go on to display their very own superpower, which we will explore in Chapter 2. When people come together to transform results, under the right conditions created by their leader, their combined efforts produce people power. Great leaders with certain styles and tactics, boost people power when they build a culture focused on people, accountability, customer intimacy, and excellence, which in turn generates the flywheel effect. Thereafter, the application of smart power and staying power sustain and compound the performance.

Amazon's story began with passion and ingenuity – the personal power, staying power and smart power of a leader, who went on to apply goal and process power to design the unique customer experience. The Amazon flywheel accelerated when people power was amplified by culture power embodied in the principles of:

Customer Obsession: We start with the customer and work backwards.

Innovation: If you don't listen to your customers you will fail. But if you only listen to your customers you will also fail.

Bias for Action: We live in a time of unheralded revolution and insurmountable opportunity – provided we make every minute count.

Ownership: Ownership matters when you're building a great company. Owners think long-term, plead passionately for their projects and ideas, and are empowered to respectfully challenge decisions.

High Hiring Bar: When making a hiring decision we ask ourselves: "Will I admire this person? Will I learn from this person? Is this person a superstar?"

Frugality: We spend money on things that really matter and believe that frugality breeds resourcefulness, self-sufficiency, and invention!

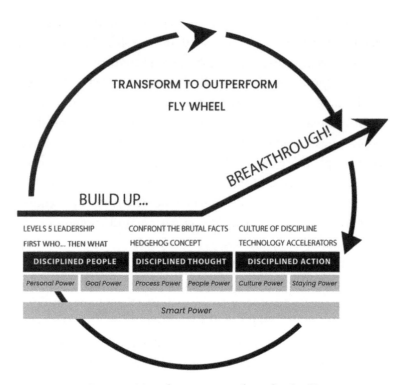

Figure 4: Transform to outperform flywheel[7]

Displaying superpower

We tend to find our heroes in the world of sport and celebrity and occasionally in the guise of a colleague, leader, family member, or neighbour when they inspire us with a special talent, a courageous act, or a story of triumph over hardship; they fill us with hope and make us want to be better people. Then there are superheroes who pursue an extraordinary vision, reinvent continuously, and outperform extraordinarily. Their destiny seems to have been charted the moment they arrived in the world. These people stand out for their longevity, persistence, their displays of superpower, and the ripple

---

[7] Image redrawn and adapted from Jim Collins, *Good to Great*, Random House Business Books, 2001, p. 12.

effect of their actions and personality. Their lives are evidence of the transformational potential in all of us.

One such man, imprisoned for 27 years, sacrificed much, and fused his own transformation with that of his country to release the most extraordinary consequences for humanity – a leadership performance so unique and magnificent it is without comparison.

Formative moments and awakenings

Nelson Rolihlahla Mandela was born into the Xhosa royal family on 18 July 1918 in the village of Mvezo, South Africa. His birth name Rolihlahla means 'pulling the branch of a tree' or literally 'troublemaker'. The first in his family to be educated, the Christian name Nelson was given to him at his Methodist school.

Academically successful through what he described as 'plain hard work', Nelson found work with a firm of attorneys, progressed through law studies, and graduated from Fort Hare in 1943. Accompanied by his alumni Oliver Tambo, they set up a law firm to provide free and low-cost counsel to unrepresented black people. Through friendships, Nelson joined the African National Congress (ANC) and for 20 years directed peaceful acts of defiance against the racist policies of the South African government. In March 1960, police officers opened fire on protesters in a township called Sharpeville. A total of 69 people died, 150 were wounded and many, including Mandela, were detained by police. Horrified and conceding the failure of passive resistance, he and his colleagues established *Umkhonto we Sizwe* (Spear of the Nation), an armed wing of the ANC with the goal of sabotaging government targets. In 1962, Nelson was sentenced to five years for orchestrating a three-day national workers strike. Whilst there he was tried on charges of sabotage and received a life sentence.

Mastery, reinvention, and context

Whilst incarcerated, Nelson honed his philosophy, political strengths, and ability for drama and theatre. He realized that peace and democracy would not be achieved through violence and dedicated himself to understanding and forgiving his enemies and moving towards reconciliation. He studied their language – Afrikaans – their history, culture, and coveted game of rugby. He developed immense personal and soft power to conquer his foes one by one: the prison guards, the top politicians, advisers and, finally, the whole of South Africa. After several years of discussions and under increasing international pressure, he was released in 1990, into a world where many symbols of oppression were being overturned – such as the Berlin Wall and the departure of Russian troops from Afghanistan. The combination of strengths, principles, and context released a superpower, literally capable of saving lives and changing the world.

After four years of negotiations and political tensions in which civil war was averted more than once, Nelson Mandela was elected President of South Africa in the first democratic elections. He led the country through reconciliation and atonement with a new constitution, a government based on majority rule, and a unified, discrimination-free, education system.

This story of one man's incredible life conveys the ultimate leadership challenge: to transform oneself in pursuit of an extraordinary vision and in doing so transform the behaviour and results of others.

Conclusion

Such leaders know their strengths and those of the team, help others set aside personal agendas to work for a compelling future, and provide a context in which the team deliver their highest value. This parallel development of a leader and team generates colliding moments of distinguished performance, a continuous double helix compelled by seven overarching transformation powers: personal, goal, process, people, culture, smart and staying power. Brilliant leaders transform results by transforming their team. Whilst aspiring to be brilliant, the target of our own outstanding performance may not be as noble as the reformation of a nation, but noble it will be, nonetheless. Thus, we begin our journey in the next chapter with a focus on initiating transformation with the release of personal power.

Action points

1. Determine your position (or that of your team or wider company) on the performance curve. Scan your environment and look for change triggers.
2. Reflect on your journey so far, reinvention moments, support structure, and resources.
3. Aim for outperformance, choose your competition, compare performance, and consider what it takes to win: humble leadership, the right people, confronting the facts, simplified focus that guides everything, discipline, and the seven transformative powers.
4. Extract lessons from your transformation heroes: their formative moments, awakenings, reinvention moments, and superpowers.

Chapter 2

Personal power

Introduction

Personal power is the value we create and the positive influence we have on others when we understand our strengths, personality advantages, and motivations, and use this knowledge to drive our behaviour. Hints of personal power show up early in life when the naivete and confidence of youth allow unfiltered displays of talent and personality. Some people understand the source of their power and progress rapidly to moments of superpower, some have it and lose it for a while, and for others it takes time and experience to develop. When we eventually find this power, we begin to do our best work; our success is no longer the product of raw ambition and perseverance, but is powered through our unique personality.

Wielding the SABRE

Confidence is fickle. We can be hypnotized by negative feedback, assign ourselves labels, and view them as unchangeable: 'I'm not good with numbers; I have limited potential'. Over time, labels convince us of our strengths and weaknesses, becoming hooks on which we hang our choices. In the voice of one executive:

> In my early career, I was excited and passionate. I studied hard and experienced one success after another. Along the way, something happened; I think it was the responsibility and pressure. I obsess about being judged, I call myself names, and think everyone is better than I am. The words of certain people

> really get to me, and the good days or feedback just don't compensate. I have lost my mojo; one day I rule the world, the next I am anxious and miserable. I can sense that it shows; my boss is starting to doubt me and second-guess my decisions.

Unhealthy preoccupation with perceptions and presupposition of negative judgement by others is destructive. Sometimes, despite all the good stuff, we question our abilities and opinions. This stunts our willingness to take on challenges we consider beyond our reach, and underpowers our communication. By retracing personality, we can connect the dots to reveal strengths, match this potential with motives and values, sharpen our instincts, take charge of emotions, and crystallize our opinions. According to research,[8] when we see ourselves clearly, we are more confident and creative, make sounder decisions, build stronger relationships, and communicate more effectively. We are less likely to lie, cheat, or steal. We are better workers who get more promotions and are more effective leaders. Personal power grows as we develop clarity of leadership or life philosophy and imprint on people around us in a good way. We know personal power is at play when we act from instinct, feel challenged yet capable, are confident in our goals, when others respond to us positively, and outcomes are good or better than expected.

As any aficionado of the legendary *Star Wars* series knows, the light sabre wielded by a Jedi knight and a Sith (the dark side) is a symbol of personal power, a conduit to the invisible 'force' which helps defend against the enemy. The colour of the sabre infers certain traits and mastery. Personal power is wielding your light

---

[8] Tascha Eurich, 'What self-awareness really is (and how to cultivate it)' (HBR Emotional Intelligence Series), *Harvard Business Review*, 4 January 2018. Available from https://hbr.org/2018/01/what-self-awareness-really-is-and-how-to-cultivate-it [accessed 19 May 2022].

SABRE; the power is within you – you need to find it, train it, and use it to get results.

Strengths and personality

Awareness and activation

Beliefs and values

Refresh and re-frame (beliefs, goals, and philosophy)

Engage

Figure 5: SABRE model

Through awareness of strengths and personality we discover our distinctive edge; by bringing values and beliefs into sharp focus, we reconnect with our passion and test our strengths in new ways. The knowledge and experience gradually congeal into a refreshed, conviction-filled, approach. We cannot help but powerfully influence others when we take value-adding action and communicate with authority.

In the following section we uncover what it takes to find personal power. First, we focus on the tactics for taking control of emotions and insecurities, as we go to therapy. We go on to explore the power of values and how to integrate these with our personality and strengths to reveal our best self. Finally, through the narration of our story and the building of a personal brand, we have the ingredients to convert personal power into displays of superpowers.

Finding personal power

We often overlook the crucible moments that initiate personal transformation. The following anecdote is one in a series of experiences which led me to my personal power.

Fight, flight, or freeze

As a senior HR executive in a large global company, it was an exciting time; I was responsible for a much-expanded business after a major acquisition. One day, during lunch at a board meeting, in a backhanded quip, a colleague dropped a metaphorical bomb. We resumed the meeting, and the penny began to drop. I was completely distracted, my mind detonated into spasms of anger, as I fought to keep control. The consequences reverberated during my flight home. On landing, I called the offending colleague and unleashed an uncensored tirade. 'Why would you do such a thing without consulting others? How is this arrangement good for everyone?' I was enraged and incapable of responding any other way. 'I could tell I'd upset you', he responded, attempting appeasement. Having none of it, I ended the call. Feeling betrayed and convinced of the impact, I decided I would resign rather than support the arrangement. The colleague had casually revealed a plan for organizational change that he had stealthily influenced in the background, and which would impact several people; a change that would provide him advantages and disregard impacts on others.

I was in fight mode, consumed with a feeling of injustice, beneath which lurked the usual fear that I was not good enough. I was challenged to the boundaries of experience and oppressed by my internal critic, which demanded perfection and gnawed at my confidence. My prized career and fragile self-esteem were under threat. At least, that's the reaction my subconscious chose. In a second, emotions were high, my heart pumped fast, and I could think of nothing else. Our mind's reaction to something which threatens to undermine our dignity or self-esteem can be deeply painful. In *Man's Search for Meaning*, the psychotherapist Victor Frankl describes how, when beaten by concentration camp guards, the pain came not from the blow itself but from the unreasonableness and unjustness of it all.[9] This 'fight, flight, or freeze' stress response is an unconscious reaction in the amygdala, the primitive part of our brain which evolved to protect us from wild animals and is hardwired to ensure rapid action for survival. It draws information from our unconscious, decides we are in crisis, and changes physiology. Quickened breathing increases oxygen. Adrenaline and hormones despatched around the body make us faster and

---

[9] Victor E. Frankl, *Man's Search for Meaning*, Random House, 2004 (1959), p. 36.

stronger. Blood supply is diverted to the limbs and vital organs and away from the thinking brain; we literally can't think straight as too much rational thinking would slow us down.

After a weekend of reflection, I consulted a colleague with a knack for telling it how it is. 'Understand your position of influence here', he advised. Through his help, a review of achievements, strengths, and values, I took hold of my narrative, and rediscovered my highest distinct value and personal power. Amid major change, I had lost sight of this. I was able to steer through this awkward strait, redress the situation, and withdraw from an emotionally charged situation with the notorious plan reconfigured. The period of personal transformation that followed meant I would never again feel, behave, or react that way. The adversity proved a turning point, a time of personal growth, during which I encountered some of my finest moments. Steadfast in my desire to resolve crises of confidence, I perfected the approach for use in coaching others. I find everyone benefits immensely from running their 'tapes', refreshing perspective and rediscovering personal power.

Go to therapy

In the offending situation, I entered what can be termed 'the trance of self-doubt'. It was during intense introspection and self-hypnosis that I was able to see straight. I went on to study therapy techniques and was amazed by their revolutionary impact. I am now an advocate for brief therapy to support mental wellness. It's a form of psychological coaching with special techniques for helping people get out of their own way. Soon enough, therapy will be a mainstream intervention at work, as companies accept its power to support performance. Winning sports teams know this already. There are moments in people's lives and careers when working with a professional coach, therapist, or mentor helps re-frame the meaning of experience and reinvigorate future focus and wellbeing.

Diminish the power of the inner critic

When coaching others, I find it's the stuff inside that wreaks havoc. Fragile self-esteem, perfectionism, stress, and overthinking create vicious self-critique, worse than anything another person might inflict. This inner voice is designed to keep us safe but if it's too harsh we bury ourselves in self-doubt and predict self-fulfilling bad outcomes. We need to appreciate its protective benefits and neutralize its negative power. Using therapy techniques, I was able to transform thinking patterns and background chatter. I grew self-assured, able to curtail negative self-talk. Situations, frustrations, and toxic people could no longer undermine my identity. Still a fellow struggler and work in progress, not immune from the perils of the inner voice or critique of others, I have shortcomings which disappoint me, although I now discriminate between protective internal talk and noise. I have embedded empowering beliefs. This mindset prepared me to lead through challenging times, to resist ego, and stay focused on external factors. I developed confidence in my judgement, clear vision, and the capacity to think bigger, find solutions, and influence effectively.

Recognize the trance of self-doubt

You may be surprised to learn that 90% of our day takes place in one trance or another, often triggered by our routines or our thoughts.[10] When we drive on autopilot, for instance, a thought occurs and off we go down a rabbit hole; the unconscious mind continues to maintain peripheral vision until we arrive home surprised and unable to recall the journey. Trance is an altered state of consciousness in which attention is narrowed, focused exclusively on a train of thought. In this state we become highly suggestible as

---

[10] Trevor Silvester, *Cognitive Hypnotherapy: What's That About and How Can I Use It?* Matador/Troubador Publishing Ltd., 2010, p. 27.

our unconscious mind listens, feeds off our imagination and the story we tell ourselves, and stores information for future use. In the trance of self-doubt, we misidentify with unproductive beliefs, e.g. 'I am not capable enough'. The unconscious mind generates a stress response to protect us. The behaviours and emotions result in doing things that, to our conscious self, are unhelpful. Our trances and their styles tend to repeat, like skills. They are where we make our life the way it is, where we achieve peak and poor performance![11] Scientists are increasingly aware of the nature of the trance state.[12] In summary, during a state of trance, we experience brain wave and brain activity changes; we are tuned in to our emotional memories and imagination; information can be downloaded into our subconscious and associations made, without the interference of rational thought. Trance moments are so natural to us that we don't realize they are happening.[13]

Diffuse the trance

The trance of self-doubt is particularly unhelpful, so we need to diffuse it or replace it with a positive alternative. Look out for moments of daydreaming or negative feelings and destructive behaviours to find trance moments. Identify your style: do you forget everything that happened, do you read the minds of others, do you imagine worst-case scenarios? These are hints of trance. By noticing the style or phenomenon by which you operate, e.g. amnesia, hallucinations, mind reading, you can begin to untangle

---

[11] Stephen Wolinsky, *Trances People Live: Healing Approaches in Quantum Psychology*, Bramble Books, 1991, p. 19.

[12] Mark P. Jensen, Tomonori Adachi, and Shahin Hakimian, 'Brain oscillations, hypnosis, and hypnotizability', *The American Journal of Clinical Hypnosis*, 2015;57(3): 230–253. Available from www.ncbi.nlm.nih.gov/pmc/articles/PMC4361031/ [accessed 19 May 2022].

[13] Stephen Wolinsky, *Trances People Live: Healing Approaches in Quantum Psychology*, Bramble Books, 1991, pp. 19–28.

the trance. Deploy my SOBER and KIND process below, adjust your language, and demonstrate self-compassion. Work with a cognitive hypnotherapist, if possible. The trance process is powerful and can bring about peak performance. Just as our minds are suggestible to negative chatter, they are receptive to positive guiding states that empower us.

SOBER and KIND process

Scenario	Identify the scenario and the stimulus. There is usually a pattern to the situations that trigger the problem. When does the problem occur? What similarities exist between situations?
Observe	Observe what happens to you as if you were another person looking on. What process do you follow? Break it into steps. See through someone else's eyes. 'How would my spouse, best friend, or boss analyse this?'
Behaviour and Beliefs	Break down behaviours and try to understand beliefs driving behaviour. Ask 'What is the positive intention of the behaviour? What do I expect to happen as a result of the behaviour? Why is this important to me?'
Emotion	Notice the emotions as distinct from behaviour and identify the cause. There are often two or three emotions. Analyse the reason why the emotion occurs and decide whether the emotion is a suitable response.

Results	Observe the consequences. 'When does the behaviour stop? What conditions exist to make it stop? How do others react? How do I feel?'
Kind	Treat yourself with kindness and respect as you would a friend. Each time the need for critique surfaces, replace it with constructive self-talk. Instead of 'you idiot', use 'You're trying hard; you are resilient'. This can feel fake at first; you have spent years convincing yourself, so the belief may be ingrained. A change in language reduces the power of the critique.
Invite Change	Being open and excited about change generates growth and resilience. Don't fight the change; seek it out, so it never catches you out.
New Beliefs	Better beliefs help you recover from the addiction to negativity. Start with a couple and build evidence to support your new belief until you are utterly convinced.
Determination (to change)	The final step is the commitment to change. Discuss your plan with a coach, family member, colleague, or boss to increase commitment to act. Dissect the cause and effect of situations and develop new beliefs; make them real with dedication and persistence. Change may seem invisible at first, but something unexpected will reveal that transformation has happened.

Adopt empowering beliefs

The following beliefs tone down negative emotions for many people. A belief is not a mantra; it has to be a genuine belief to make the difference.

- ❖ 'Nothing turns out as bad as I think.' When anxiety brings catastrophic thinking, this belief can bring us down from the ledge, switch off the emotional centre, and engage the rational brain.

- ❖ 'I am not the centre of everything; this is not about me.' Our paranoid tendency to think that everything is aimed at us triggers the inner critic and the trance of self-doubt. By remembering this belief, responses become more rational, leaving our minds free to engage.

- ❖ 'I have unlimited potential and can do anything I want to.' Refusing to accept the limitations we or others place on us allows access to our creativity and ability to do things we never thought possible.

- ❖ 'I am in charge of my destiny, and I can find the resources.' Taking ownership and adopting an internal locus of control stops us waiting for others to decide the future or blaming others when something doesn't go our way.

- ❖ 'I can leave a positive impression on others no matter how difficult the message.' There is always a way to deal with others that leaves them feeling you've added value, even when the subject of the interaction is negative. Recognizing these forces helps you to find better strategies for responding.

- ❖ 'There is always another way.' Staying open and primed for alternatives ensures we never feel blocked.

- ❖ 'There is no such thing as failure, just feedback.' Substituting the idea of failure for continuous improvement makes us curious and productive.

Find beliefs that work for you. They don't have to be fact, just plausible, believed by you, and helpful to you.

Focus outward

Conversely, stop thinking about yourself or the impact on yourself; focusing outward lets you see the bigger picture. Mental energy focused inward increases turmoil, reduces flexibility, and isolates you. Notice everything outside of yourself, seek harmony with the environment, and prime your mind to see connections or alternatives. Adapt to events, read the weather, and adjust the plan. If you try to dominate the environment or push against the natural course, it may overwhelm you. Notice detail and appreciate everything; drop the tendency for dissatisfaction. Learn to see the good in the small and the bigger things. Develop a mission, a reason for doing what you do; look to your values for the answer to what's important.[14]

Master continually

Recognize and relax into skills and competencies you've mastered; you didn't get where you are without them. You don't always have to prove yourself. A relaxed approach lets your unconscious mind draw from your experience. Treat feedback as a gift; invite it, acknowledge it, and appreciate it. Continue to develop. As the world changes, the target moves so we need to update. If you don't feel masterful, work on improving skills in your chosen field to build confidence.

Take action

Change happens when we envision a future and act on it. Design your life, plan for balance between career, family, and social life,

---

[14] Alex Pattakos, *Prisoners of Our Thoughts*, Berrett-Koehler Inc, 2010, pp. 143–172.

and choose ways to make it happen. Set personal goals with clear outcomes. Create an image in the mind for you to chase. Act, with daily intentions; a goal without action is squandered. Explore new solutions, be prepared to put aside strong ideas, and find alternatives.

Create a scorecard and dashboard

Create a scorecard to capture personal transformation goals and a dashboard to provide a snapshot of the latest data. Use a spreadsheet, smart app, or whatever works for you. When we measure something, it piques motivation, and encourages action. We enjoy being in control, competing against our best performance. Start with one or two goals in each focus area. Use time, quantity or quality-based targets, and a simple tracker to get used to the routine of daily checking and follow-up action. Once a habit has formed, build on the habit, and add a new data point. Add indicators from your fitness tracker if you have one – steps, sleep, nutrition, weight, or other indicators of well-being. If you have access to medical records, you can include health measures like blood pressure readings, resting heart rate, cholesterol, and weight so that you become accustomed to what's normal for you.

Consult the compass

We all have values that guide us, albeit often buried in our unconscious; they serve as a personal compass and affect our emotions, behaviours, how we derive meaning from life, and our underlying happiness. When in congruence with values we feel contented and fulfilled. Conversely, we feel lost or inauthentic in conflict. I have learned to revisit values when I feel persistent discomfort. List, compare, and rank values in order of importance; work out the benefit or purpose of each value and consider the extent to which they are currently satisfied in and out of work. When we realize that violated values are the root of discontent, it motivates us to shape better life experience and change direction.

Values and motives

Leaders report the process of uncovering values to be revealing and inspiring. The values they describe are endless; however, psychologists gravitate towards ten values, identified by Shalom Schwartz.[15] It is possible to find people who endorse them in every culture:

1. Power.
2. Security – the value that people place on safety, security, stability, harmony, and order – in their own lives, their relationships with others, and society at large.
3. Self-direction – being able to make your own decisions.
4. Hedonism – pursuit of pleasure, self-indulgence.
5. Tradition – respect for the customs and ideas of your culture.
6. Achievement.
7. Conformity – not doing things that might violate social norms or upset others.
8. Stimulation or excitement.
9. Benevolence – taking care of people you know personally.
10. Universalism – protecting the welfare of all people, whether you know them or not, as well as caring for animals and nature.

---

[15] Shalom H. Schwartz, 'An overview of the Schwartz theory of basic values', *Online Readings in Psychology and Culture*, 2012, 2(1). https://doi.org/10.9707/2307-0919.1116

Value questions

To increase awareness of your values, answer searching questions and discuss them with a colleague or friend. Capture your results. Run a search online for value words that resonate.

- ❖ What are you passionate about?
- ❖ What behaviours and actions frustrate or upset you?
- ❖ What interests do you have or what are you curious about?
- ❖ What is most important to you?
- ❖ Why do you do what you do?
- ❖ What memorable lessons from your parents do you recognize today?
- ❖ What have been your high-impact life events; what did each one teach you?
- ❖ What lessons have you learned from other people, teachers, bosses etc.?
- ❖ When are your happiest moments in life and why?

Personal goal analysis

Personal goals are motivated by and provide the best opportunity to live in alignment with values. Follow these steps to tease out goal-based values for action planning.

1. Brainstorm a long list of life and career goals.
2. Prioritize the goals – identify the top three to five. A blend of career, family, and personal works well.
3. What is the outcome of each of the goals? What will this give you? Why is this important?
4. Take each goal and pan out to a time in the future when the goal has been achieved. Imagine a day in your life after achieving the goal and describe what you feel, see, and hear happening around you. Then ask again what the

goal is giving you. What purpose is it serving? Why is this important?

5.   Work backwards from the outcome to the present day; consider the steps and the learning necessary to get to the outcome. What will you value most about the journey and why?

Values that appear frequently in connection with the priority goals indicate importance. Studies demonstrate that wellbeing is strongly influenced by the type of values a person lives by, and that intrinsic values like learning and team spirit are more beneficial to wellbeing than extrinsic values like pay and status.[16] Increasing awareness of values at key moments releases personal power and increases happiness. By emphasizing the journey to a goal rather than the goal itself, you can rebalance excessive focus on extrinsic values.

Amplify personality

Personality is how we sum up ourselves and others, a blend of traits, genetics, values, culture, experience, and psychology which shows up inside our heads and as perceived by others. Our identity evolves with experience and emotional events; moments of pride, shame, and realization; the times we are praised, supported, or chastised. We easily recognize influences of adulthood but are often blinded by disproportionately influential childhood experiences; events processed by a thirsty young brain which did not have full reasoning capacity until our twenties, and which may have misplaced a message or two. Incidents from our early years reveal clues to our drive, the reasons we behave as we do, and the causes of empowering and limiting beliefs, which affect our choices. During my process of discovery, I found moments of childhood embarrassment

---

[16] Hugo Alberts, 'A coaching masterclass on meaning and valued living', Positive Psychology Program BV, 2018.

or anxiety lurking near the surface. Being singled out for not wearing the new school uniform and other moments connected with social status. Events that were undoubtedly important to my younger self. My husband insists these memories are to blame for a wardrobe, overstocked with clothes and shoes! I dredged up the advice of teachers and bosses, whose impact I understand retrospectively. I recognized how my personality was shaped by family life and working amongst adults from age 11. I recalled the gruelling schedule of hospitality work, the camaraderie, rituals, and culture of work. I realized it's where I learned about people – hard workers, oddballs, good and bad managers – and the challenges of mobilizing people to get work done. The suicide of a parent at 17 years old, followed by a stint working alone in a foreign country, were distinct moments of reinvention.

As fascinating as personality is, how can we then understand and amplify it?

Measure personality

Do you act the same way when socializing with friends or sitting in a formal meeting with the boss at work? Consider notable events in your life that caused you to make different choices or feel as if you changed. You will notice that your personality evolves and differs according to circumstance. No person acts the same all the time; flexibility is required to get through life. We do however repeat tendencies over time, some of which are shared with everyone as part of human nature, and others which are unique to us; these little differences make a big difference in our lives. The building blocks of personality include our traits and orientations, social or outward-facing motivation, internal psychological motivation, and our emotional intensity. We fall somewhere along a continuum of traits and motives which varies according to the context we face. Our personality is encapsulated and expressed through our verbal and non-verbal communication.

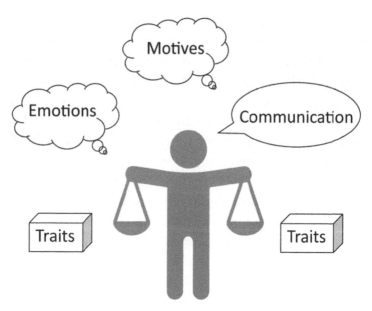

Figure 6: Building blocks of personality

The *Big Five* are traits considered to have most impact on personality: extroversion, neuroticism, agreeableness, conscientiousness, and openness.

Social motivation is an internal state that directs behaviour towards or away from specific outcomes; it can change in different stages of our life. The varying need for affiliation, achievement, and power account for personality differences.

Psychological motivation operates entirely inside our head, controlling thoughts and emotions, and maintains a comfortable psychological state, namely: consistency, self-esteem, and authenticity.

Emotions – negative and positive affectivity are the tendency to experience positive and negative emotions, and at what intensity. For more details visit transformtooutperform.com.

We think we own the truth about ourselves because we have the inside story on what happens in our head. Our view, however, is only one-dimensional; research shows that self-assessments aren't often accurate.[17] You have probably completed a personality test at some time. Such tools are built on extensive behavioural data that identify traits correlated with success and attempt to indicate how a person might act. You may recognize the *Big Five* or any of the motives in your results. Assessments use 'types' as shorthand to box everyone into a small number of personality descriptors; however, there are no true types. People do not fall naturally or cleanly into one category or another, and the results are only a guide.

Explore your personality to access personal power. Free assessments are available online and your human resources team may provide tools. The value is in careful reflection on the data and a follow-up plan. Compare your perception with the outcome of the assessment; don't accept findings at face value or dismiss them out of hand. Reconcile the results with the views of people who know you and consider features you are blind to. Summarize key learnings. If you are unhappy with a feature of your personality, commit to modifying it and plan how you can do this over time. Review current behaviours against motives, particularly where you have difficulty understanding your decisions. Assess what may be driving that behaviour.

Summon strengths

It's exhilarating to hear someone tell us what we are good at. A strength described by an objective observer is magnified and we are more inclined to accept it. We feel legitimized, fluff out our feathers, and seek opportunities to display more. Without this validation, we may struggle to see our traits or skills as strengths; we know too well the inner workings of our mind, the confidence and competence gaps, and the effort it takes to perform. Negative

---

[17] Mark Leary, *Why You Are Who You Are: Investigations into Human Personality*, The Great Courses, 2018.

criticism is easier to believe – it reinforces paranoia and roots in our memory. We may hide our weakness to preserve our emotional self or, worse, become defensive, resistant, and try to fit in to a role we are not suited to. The following case study highlights the risk of failing to match skills and strengths with our role and purpose.

Mismatched strengths

A brilliant design engineer in a manufacturing company had an ability to develop practical innovations and contributed to the company's most successful products. He was famous for his ability to get lost in a technical challenge and work long hours to reach 'eureka' moments. His enthusiasm for work was intense and infectious. The company were so impressed they promoted him to a management role. Very soon he began to face problems. His brilliant design skills were suppressed by meetings, people issues, and operational challenges, which he handled awkwardly. His boss sent him on training courses to develop personal impact, people management, and commercial skills. His creative, technical strengths and introverted focus were deemed weaknesses in the new role. He was not a strong manager and appeared stubborn and disengaged. In time, the respect he had enjoyed in the company dwindled away. He failed and left.

The surprising reality is that a focus on strengths increases productivity and performance. Emphasizing weakness dampens productivity; it's never where we will perform our best. A CLC study revealed that formal and informal performance reviews with an emphasis on strengths had a 36% and 26% increase in performance, respectively, whilst a focus on weakness in the formal and informal reviews had a 27% and 11% decrease.[18] High engagement

---

[18] Corporate Leadership Council, *Building the High-Performance Workforce*, 2002.

levels at work are directly correlated with our ability to use our talents and be our best self. Awareness of strengths alone does not create success; the process of learning how to use them better and acting upon the learning makes the difference.

Giving and receiving feedback

Your ability to give, receive, and process feedback is central to your development. Connections will strengthen when you practise giving the gift of thoughtful feedback to others. Develop the ability to receive feedback gracefully, thanking a person for feedback and asking clarifying questions without defensiveness. Accept and corroborate information with supporting evidence; turn it into a learning moment or disregard it without obsessing over it.

Feedback friends

Work with individuals who will provide candid and supportive feedback. You will be blind to aspects of your style and personality.

1. Allow the person time to think and frame the feedback. Offer descriptive feedback on their own contribution or describe a positive way in which they impact you or others. Genuine thoughtful feedback, not gushing compliments; imprint and activate their desire for reciprocity.
2. Show you value their judgement and ask about situations in which you made an important contribution. Ask what you did, your impact on others, and how to use the strength more.
3. Assemble feedback into themes of skills, behaviours, traits, or competencies. Describe the theme in a single statement.
4. Identify current dilemmas and explore how these strengths might be applied to solving them. Uncover new ways of responding to situations that show you at your best.

5. Make a short action plan to develop and increase the use of strengths. Limit the number of actions to ensure you will do it.

6. Using personality and strengths information, write a narrative about yourself to reinforce understanding, insights, and strengthen your sense of self. *When I am at my best, I do this because…; I tend to…; my biggest contribution is…; I see how this connects in my life because…; my underpinning motives are…; my core values are…; my mission is…; my vision is…; I intend to…*

Martin Seligman, the founder of positive psychology in his book *Flourish*, describes two exercises which resulted in sustained benefits for individuals.[19] The first is identification of signature strengths and the act of scheduling time to exercise one or more of the strengths in a new way. The second is an exercise of purposefully writing down three things that went well today and why. Go online to www.authentichappiness.org and register free to complete the Values in Action Signature Strengths test and obtain a list of signature strengths. A strengths narrative forms the foundation of your story which adapts over time, particularly following moments of transition and reinvention.

Narrate your story

Too often we leave our story to chance or let others create it for us. Getting out of our own way means taking control of our narrative. Start now by compiling your story in a dynamic portable resume with a dashboard of data which captures strengths, learning, achievements, assessments, and career plan.

---

[19] Martin Seligman, *Flourish: A New Understanding of Happiness and Well Being and How to Achieve Them*, Nicholas Brealey Publishing, 2011.

Calibrate competence

Unpack and capture experience, achievements, and leadership skills, and assess transformational impact. Focus first on recent experiences for relevance and delve deeper for critical career incidents. What was the:

1. situation or context; what was happening at the time?
2. scale in terms of financial and human resources and the implications?
3. task or tasks to be completed?
4. complexity or challenge in addition to scale, the unique characteristics, and issues they caused?
5. action taken by you (and your team)?
6. tangible outcome achieved and impact on others (capture unsatisfactory performances)?
7. learning, transformation or reinvention, and the lasting impact?

Categorize competencies, experiences, leadership styles, and skills. Watch out for strengths that show up regularly. Highlight unsatisfactory moments or performances. A balanced perspective on failures and performance gaps increases authenticity and ensures future experiences are planned to fill gaps.

Elevator speech

Using the information gathered, find ways of concisely describing yourself. Use short dynamic statements which summarize projects and progress. The exercise resurfaces experience, increases the ability to draw from it in new situations, strengthens your results focus, and creates new learning. Use the following questions to increase impact.

What problem am I solving for the business, my boss, my team?

Which performance/experience examples support this solution?

What makes me uniquely positioned to do this?

What new ideas or innovations have I brought?

What do I do at my best?

What skills and experience have I mastered?

How does this support future performance?

Compile your own info graphic and represent information visually. Think of it as your publicity or brand document.

Build your brand

Fascinating people are more successful, have more friends and followers, and make more money. Do you have a fascinating personal or leadership brand? Your friends, colleagues, or parents would probably select consistent adjectives to describe you: driven, comical, caring, clever perhaps. They will know what's important to you, your passions and strengths. Your team will describe your style, what you expect in terms of performance, and how you view the world. A personal or leadership brand is a reputation which vividly communicates principles, success behaviours, and strengths for which you are instantly recognized; the highest value you add. Leaders and employees who recognize the power of their brand elevate their profile within an organization.

Vivid brand image

A brand is exciting when it reveals more of who you are; the authentic you, not an artificial persona. When you speak with conviction, vision, and principles you create curiosity in others. Followers identify and connect with your brand; it makes them feel significant and leads to their own growth. Richard Branson and his Virgin brand communicate creativity and breaking through tradition. Originally, Branson set up his mail-order record business and Virgin record stores but later disrupted many stale industries: air travel, rail travel, finance. He once said, 'There is no point starting your own business unless you do it out of a sense of frustration'. He is a shy and understated person, renowned for a fresh and fun approach, for being adventurous, passionate, and for his integrity. His style is embedded in the Virgin group and is present every time he engages publicly.

EMBRACE SELF is my system to help develop a personal and leadership brand.

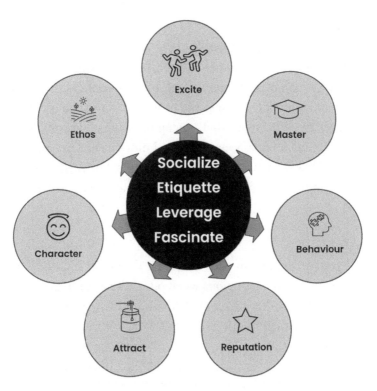

Figure 7: EMBRACE SELF system

Excite

A pattern or system.

Our ability to call on our experience is what generates career progression and qualifies us to lead, make decisions, and advise others. No person experiences the world in the same way as the next, each having a nuanced and unique take on things. When you notice people responding to you, seeking your advice or help, it's time to maximize the value of your experience to others by packaging it into a proprietary system or pattern. Develop a method, record it, give it a name or an acronym, and build content, case studies and illustrative stories to inspire, influence, and excite followers.

Master

Strengths

Strengths are key: what we do, how we do it, and how it is distinct from the next person. Much of our distinctiveness is personality, comprising our unique life experiences, personal beliefs, and genetics. It's possible to mimic a personality but it can never be truly replicated. Recognizing that personality is our unique advantage, we must reveal more of it. This uniqueness, blended with other strengths like skills, knowledge, experience, and thinking style applied in a balanced way, creates our brand.

Mastery

Being recognized as a master or expert is the brand ambition. We become masters or champions when our skill has been practised and perfected to the degree that it's committed to the unconscious and encoded in our neural network. We must commit to continuous application and growth of strengths to build mastery. A study by Anders Ericsson in 1993 identified that mastery comes with 10,000 hours of deliberate practice combined with expert coaching.[20]

Behaviour
Brand building
Certain behaviours build a brand, whilst others can damage it. The emphasis may depend upon the culture and values of a business. Competencies which build leadership reputation include:

- ❖ strategy and innovation – challenges the current paradigm, brings thought leadership, is market savvy and analytical;
- ❖ collaboration – builds constructive internal and external partnerships;
- ❖ breakthrough results – consistently delivers strong results and occasional breakthrough;
- ❖ business and functional agility – is commercially agile, operationally astute, and professionally expert;
- ❖ people development – acknowledges strengths, effort, and results; provides supportive feedback, coaches, mentors, and sponsors learning;
- ❖ inspirational – is values driven, humble, authentic, and courageous.

Brand damaging
Behaviours which derail leaders or damage reputation when used in excess include:

- ❖ being, emotional, political, territorial, and parochial;

---

[20] K. Anders Ericsson, Ralf T. Krampe, and Clemens Tesch-Römer, 'The role of deliberate practice in the acquisition of expert performance', *Psychological Review*, 1993;100(3): 363. https://psycnet.apa.org/buy/1993-40718-001

❖ failing to get behind difficult decisions made by the leadership team;

❖ resisting change and progress;

❖ defensiveness, pessimism, and negativity;

❖ inconsistency in practice or the treatment of others;

❖ using customers, suppliers, or others as an excuse for inflexibility. 'My customer won't accept this change';

❖ selective responsiveness and failing to deliver on commitments;

❖ acting to conceal or lacking transparency;

❖ disparaging the reputation of other colleagues, business units, or teams.

Reputation

Values alignment

As a leader, your brand and values must integrate with those of the organization. Identify and remedy conflicts; if the values of the business conflict with yours, find a way to coexist with integrity or decide whether the current situation is sustainable.

Ethics

People can have different moral foundations and ethics, some of which arise from cultural differences. Researchers generally agree that we judge whether behaviour is morally right or wrong based on one or more of six basic moral dimensions: care, fairness, loyalty, authority, purity, and sanctity. The background to these dimensions may be founded on varying beliefs and create differences in opinion. For example, we may hold different views on things like same-sex marriage, abortion, smacking children. Ethics and morals are fraught with interpretation challenges. To protect the integrity of your personal and leadership brand use this list as a guide:

Principles	Trust, respect, responsible, fairness, caring, citizenship.
Golden rule	Treat others as you want to be treated (underpinned by the ethical principles).
Publicity	What would the outcome or action look like as headlines in the news or social media?
Parents over shoulder	What would your parents think of your behaviour if they were watching?
Universal applicability	If everyone did it, would it be a good thing?
Stakeholder impact	To what extent have people been helped/ harmed by your action?
Commercial integrity	Are commercial dealings transparent? If in doubt, debate it out.

Attract

Community

An entrepreneur must connect to an ideal client. A leader must attract and inspire their team and extended team. Knowing who you want to attract and inspire ensures your message lands where you want. A strong brand with clear principles and values influences and connects with like-minded people and impacts widely. To refine your target community and brand, ask who you want to attract, why you care, how you would like to be described by your fans, and what legacy you would like to leave.

Communication

Without communication there is no brand. Communication occurs through action, inaction, behaviour, and written and verbal communication. Consistency in communication is highly visible and accelerates impact. My favourite tool is the Fascinate assessment created by Sally Hogshead.[21] Using the science of branding, it analyses the triggers you initiate in other people through communication and provides insight into your primary and secondary personality advantages expressed as one of the seven Fascination advantages: Innovation, Power, Prestige, Passion, Trust, Mystique, and Alert.

Character

Philosophy, opinions, conviction, and boundaries
To attract followers there must be a vision or promise of the future backed by principles, a philosophy, or ideology – something to believe in. To sustain followership the brand must be underpinned by actions, beliefs, and opinions with conviction. It must communicate boundaries: what is acceptable and what is not. Followers are drawn to many things: shared values, innovation, talent, the prospect of a better life, the idea of doing something of service to others, the fulfilment of hope, the protection of their lives and families, the promise of greatness or personal growth, relief from their current circumstances, frustration, or injustice. What is your philosophy? What values and motives drive you? What is your style and why? What do you believe strongly? How do you convey this in your words and behaviour? How consistent are you? What are your opinions on a range of matters and why? What is non-negotiable to you; what won't you accept? In what way do you have a counterintuitive or different perspective? Why is this attractive (or not) to others? Consider how you communicate your philosophy.

---

[21] Sally Hogshead, *How the World Sees You: Discover Your Highest Value Through the Science of Fascination*, HarperCollins, 2014.

Ethos
Performance/adding value
It's one thing to have strengths and attributes, but it's another to use them to achieve consistent great results. If Nike failed to consistently produce quality apparel or comfortable performance-enhancing running shoes, customers would not return. The brand must perform and add value to followers in some way. Be clear about ethos and how the brand differentiates, performs, and adds value to a client, team member, or boss. Routine actions and consistently upheld principles, standards, and behaviours reinforce a personal brand.

Contribution
A brand that contributes to the wellbeing of its community and the world at large creates a legacy and sense of contribution which outlives the brand owner. Martin Seligman,[22] in his pursuit of what makes human beings flourish, has been able to underline, based on scientific evidence, something that has been part of the mantra of many great philosophers for thousands of years: human beings achieve happiness when acting in the service of others, when they feel they are making a difference to mankind. Assess your brand to determine how it serves.

Socialize
There is no brand without socialization. The actions we take, our behaviour, and the quality of results we achieve are our most powerful and authentic advert, but these can only take us so far. Big brands traditionally achieved status by spending millions on advertising and socializing to extend reach. Such grand budgets are inaccessible to most of us. Fortunately, social media has democratized

---

[22] Martin Seligman, *Flourish: A New Understanding of Happiness and Well-Being - and How to Achieve Them*, Nicholas Brealey Publishing, 2011, p. 12.

marketing and it's now easier to take control of image and achieve influencer status with the click of a button. Whilst not a fan or user of social media because of its negative impacts, I do appreciate its positive marketing power when used responsibly. Carefully design a website and selectively invest in the best social media to attract your audience.

Etiquette

How we deal with our clients, employees, and stakeholders influences reputation and whether people want to work with us. Etiquette, our manners and respect shown, is a sign of our values. How long does it take to respond to a call or query? How do we show respect for the time and investment of stakeholders? How do we work to understand and support their needs? Define your standards of etiquette, audit your performance, and take action to address any issues. Work hard to ensure every interface and interaction leaves the desired impact.

Leverage

Know what leverage you have and use it. Networks and associations built over time are important resources. Take advantage of connections to access talent, get your work recognized, and extend reach. The relationships you have developed often include like-minded people, supporters, or potential clients. Pick your moments to connect with colleagues and friends and ensure a positive reciprocal arrangement, where all parties see the benefit of the connection.

Fascinate

Finally, fascinate your followers. A brand fascinates in a variety of ways; it may pique interest through innovation, prestige appeal, passion, or other factors. To understand your own and your brand advantages, consult the work of Sally Hogshead – her books, *Fascinate*[23] and *How the World Sees You*[24] fabulously demystify brand impact. Find out how and when you trigger the right reactions in your followers. Use this knowledge to increase your impact.

Finally, having completed the six steps to personal power, we can confidently wield the SABRE and begin the quest for superpower.

From personal power to superpower

We are all creatures of transformation; our physiology and brain are designed to adapt and transform as we live and learn. Then there are transformation heroes and superheroes: those individuals whose every act, often from an early age, seems destined to lead them to greatness. These people display such purpose in life, confidence in their capabilities, and a staying power which helps them navigate struggles without losing sight of their goals. Whilst not Superman or Wonder Woman, they do appear bewitched by a divine mission; they display wisdom, conviction, an instinct for their cause or talent and, like their fictional avatars, superpowers. A life experience or awakening inspires passionate vision. The energy of their subsequent transformation radiates onto the world and the people around them. We explored briefly the extraordinary impact of Nelson Mandela in Chapter 1; Steve Jobs, founder of Apple Inc., is another transformation superhero.

---

[23] Sally Hogshead, *Fascinate: Your 7 Triggers to Persuasion and Captivation: Unlocking the Secret Triggers of Influence, Persuasion, and Captivation*, HarperCollins, 2016.
[24] Sally Hogshead, *How the World Sees You: Discover Your Highest Value Through the Science of Fascination*, HarperCollins, 2014.

Signs of superpower

Steve Jobs was captivated by his first computer at age 12. His youthful audaciousness propelled him towards a series of formative experiences: a visit to NASA, where he spied an early time-sharing terminal, a cheeky call to Bill Packard followed by a summer job, awareness of the embryonic internet, and the idea that a computer would become a communication tool. When he happened upon a piece of research in Scientific American, his course was set. Researchers measured the efficiency of locomotion in humans compared with other species. The results demonstrated the relative inefficiency of humans; that is, until the addition of a bicycle enabled humans to outperform the fastest of the selected species. Right then, Steve Jobs' appreciation for humans as creators of tools that amplify their performance launched his vision for the development of personal computing devices as an extension of the person. With uncompromising conviction, he pursued this passion and changed the world.

Like every great superhero, such talent attracts polarizing perspectives, with fanatical support at one end of the spectrum and accusations of arrogance, eccentricity, or stubbornness at the other. Whilst having achieved the extraordinary, they are as human as the rest of us, and often wrestle with insecurities or weaknesses which threaten their very being. With the benefit of hindsight, we get a clearer view of their superior performance and occasionally their 'kryptonite'. Margaret Thatcher, former UK Prime Minister, is one such transformation superhero. No person better exemplifies polarized popularity. Her political theatre, conviction, and unwavering courage delivered a contribution revered as world changing by her supporters yet heckled and disparaged by her detractors. Her kryptonite: the overuse of her strength, an unwillingness to concede, was seized upon by her nemesis, a group of male colleagues who could not accept the ideas and ideals of this powerful, uncompromising woman, and forced her resignation. through subversive dealing.

Unlocking superpowers

Superpowers are not just for superheroes. We can all turbo boost personal power at any time in our lives. Power is the capacity to do something, to influence and captivate others and in doing so affect their behaviours and attitudes. Personal power is the influence we achieve with our natural strengths and personality. Superpower is the extraordinary influence and ripple effects which follow our creativity and mastery in a challenging situation – the impact of creating a masterpiece or delivering a great performance.

Primal inclinations and mastery

In his book *Mastery*, Robert Greene asserts that the inclinations of those who become recognized masters are often remarkably clear in childhood.[25] These quite ordinary individuals possess a particularly deep and clear inner calling that dominates their thinking and leads them towards certain experiences and away from others. A chance encounter kick starts an apprenticeship and energizes learning. Natural motivation propels these people through moments of disruption, blockage, sudden breakthrough, and reinvention. Consequently, their skills become unconscious, and they know, use, and make connections where others can't. Whilst this is true, the failure to recognize a passion early on does not prevent growth and mastery. Greene suggests we interrogate memory for primal inclinations, recalling strong reactions to something simple when we were young; a desire to repeat an activity that we never tired of; or a subject that stimulated an unusual degree of curiosity.

---

[25] Robert Greene, *Mastery*, Profile Books Ltd, 2012, p. 25.

Having discovered our inclinations, we must value learning over anything else, go on to master our craft, and use our skills in a unique challenging context. Amongst my own rubble, I recalled a preoccupation with language, a pattern of presenting and leading at a young age, and a penchant for change and doing things differently – whether narrating the nativity as an infant, leading the school concert at primary school, producing and directing school plays, composing and leading the school in a rendition of my own Christmas carol, or entertaining classmates in regional dialects. At work I thrive on change, leading others, charting a path through transformation, or leading high-stakes communications. This is where my personality adds the most value and applies those strengths. Regardless of whether my calling is the right one, I can see the intersection of primal inclinations with life choices, career success, and personal growth, and I see more clearly those who recognized and curated them.

The supporting team

We don't get to build or display superpowers without support. The combination of circumstances, reinvention moments, life choices, and the people who are part of our circle of unknowing co-conspirators provide the platform for us to be who we want to be. When considering people who influenced you for better or worse, it's not long before the list extends into the hundreds. The people we encounter help us by opening doors, providing support, sharing their own experience, and role modelling a superior or even substandard performance. They may provide us with a moment to outperform, like a player setting up a goal for their team mate to shoot. Learning is accelerated through working with others, observing their behaviours and traits, analysing their success factors, and choosing to adapt and apply our own version. We do this unconsciously as children. I know that along the way, I adapted snippets of style, technique and skill from bosses, colleagues, and teams. I step into their shoes to see, feel, and apply aspects of their style as part of my approach. As a result, my own superpowers show up occasionally.

Modelling

Sometimes skills are learned from distant role models like famous personalities whose styles and preferences are visible for study. Alternatively, we can imagine their motivations and learnings based on what we see. It doesn't matter if our assessment is off the mark, only that the information we interpret offers a positive learning outcome. The process of modelling involves:

- ❖ clarifying why it's helpful to adopt a certain style;
- ❖ decoding a person's approach, identifying characteristics;
- ❖ getting to know the principles and thought processes which underpin action;
- ❖ asking where and how a role model learned a particular skill or trait to reveal circumstances which contributed to their level of expertise;
- ❖ inviting the person to help you model the skill.

Reinvention and internal transformation moments

Our lives are propelled by learning and the choices we do or don't make. By heightening awareness, we accelerate our transformation. Disruptive moments of any kind like changing jobs, changing boss, changing team, or a crisis provide transformation opportunities. Sometimes the most insignificant moments have the biggest impact. We must be open to the advantages presented by any situation. What new things do I, or will I, know because of this experience? What skill have I enhanced? In what way will this improve relationships or connections? What resources do I have at my disposal? How do I see myself differently? By answering these questions internal transformation begins. We feel the pleasure of learning, see ourselves as changed, and adjust the vision of our future.

Context

We are born into a context in which our passions and skills develop from the influences around us, those in society at large, our family, friends, our schools, and later our work. With a good headwind, this is where our strengths and passions flourish. It provides us with role models to emulate and unique experiences that shape character and competence. Consider how you might be different had you been born a generation or two earlier or later? What conditions exist or existed that would make your life easier or more difficult? Then there's the here and now, the moments in time when you face challenge or adversity and must respond with personality and mastery. It is the arrival of this uncertain context that provides the opportunity to pull out your superhero costume.

Agility and creativity

Displays of greatness are occasional or subtle to begin with and intensify with experience. They are most evident when we are at the 'top of our game', when we act from our deepest instincts. It's when we are most authentic, least self-conscious, and intensively focused on the task or goal. In some of the most challenging moments we step beyond the boundaries of a plan to respond to whatever hand we are dealt; we experience a flow state, an explosion of creativity, a deployment of superpower, sometimes in a context which allows us to rock the world, or our piece of it. My own moments occur when I combine transformational leadership with a performance

like a high-stakes presentation to large groups; they are characterized by deep experience, strong preparation, a sense of connection
with the audience, and a feeling of flow. Interestingly, my worst
moments also occur in the same situations, often in states of over-
preparation where I feel less authentic and fail to act on instinct.

IMPACT

Finally, this leads us to a recipe for unleashing superpower. Take
a generous portion of personal power evolved from personality and primal inclinations into strengths, add a deep, driving
passion and conviction. Seek out and process disruptive events
to build mastery. Purposefully reinvent at key moments and,
in doing so, recognize the internal mindset change. Identify
and prepare for challenging situations which demand your talents. Kick off with your skills and knowledge, feel the challenge,
respond intuitively, lose yourself in the performance, and create
extraordinary IMPACT on others.

Internal transformation – from disruptive moments

Mastery – from continuous immersion and learning

Passion and personal power – from awareness and
activation of inclinations, strengths, and personality

Agility and creativity – a flow moment, explosion of
creativity

Context – the unique circumstances for your opportunity
to deliver outstanding performance.

Team – to help you be the best you can be.

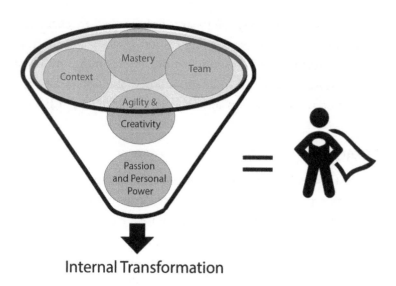

Internal Transformation

Figure 8: IMPACT model

Conclusion

Whether a leader of others or an individual contributor, releasing personal power and occasional superpower will prepare you for a lifetime of growth-inducing transformation. Let's explore now the goal power that will activate unlimited potential.

Action points

1. Become your best self, focus outward not inward, and build empowering beliefs.
2. Explore personality, your personal goals, values, and strengths. Find feedback friends.
3. Build your own dashboard, narrative, and brand.
4. Wield your SABRE, act, and influence with conviction.
5. IMPACT – combine passion and personal power. Reinvent and seek challenging opportunities to create transformational moments. Produce your own masterpiece and watch out for the ripple effects.

Chapter 3

Goal power

Introduction

By now, you have identified a need to transform, elevated your personal power, and gained a sense of what good and great personal performance look like. It's time to explore what it takes to make great team performance happen. In short, a clear purpose and reason why, a vision of what you will achieve, and goals, all wrapped up in a plan which is managed and tracked.

The why – purpose

People need to make sense out of life, particularly during challenging times when a major change can rob a person of their identity and purpose. In the absence of information and purpose, people become unproductive and dependent. The mystery created by the vacuum results in depression and smoke-signal reading. Intrigue, conspiracy theories, and anxiety abound. Victor Frankl, survivor of the Auschwitz concentration camp, and author of *Man's Search for Meaning*,[26] describes how those prisoners able to find meaning survived, whilst those who lost all hope perished. People with a powerful purpose, on the other hand, make stuff happen; they know what needs to be done without having to constantly check in; they collaborate, share responsibility, struggle together and, in doing so, form bonds that last a lifetime. When we find importance in something, we turn our attention to it, like a heat-seeking missile. The following case study illustrates how a clear purpose translates into culture and practice.

---

[26] Victor E. Frankl, *Man's Search for Meaning*, Random House, 2004 (1959), pp. 78–81.

Inspiring purpose

A revolutionary beauty company DECIEM want to change the beauty world. Their purpose, determined by their late founder Brandon Truaxe, was 'To add accountability to the beauty business' through transparency about ingredients and production costs. He was passionate about this mission, derived from the conviction that customers are getting a raw deal from the beauty industry. The company produce high-quality beauty products at a fraction of large company prices. They do everything their competitors don't do and allow their customers to influence product development. They manufacture and sell their products and are a fast-growing disruptive influence in their industry. Estée Lauder were quick to see this potential and promptly invested in the business.

To clarify team purpose, first ask:

1. What does our team do and who do we serve?
2. What problem are we trying to solve or what do we need to achieve?
3. Why are we doing this?

Repeat question 3 until you have exhausted the answers and captured the heart of what the change is about. If you arrive at something like 'to provide value for shareholders', don't stop here. Dig deeper; there will be inspiration beneath.

The what – vision

Only humans have the capacity to imagine something that does not exist and bring it into being by cooperating flexibly on a large scale. It's our imagination and the stories we share about what we dream up that connects us; the homes we live in, the places we work, culture, and religion were all created in someone's mind. When we share our vision and others believe in it, we agree rules to work by and begin creating it together. This is what we call progress and success. Ask any successful leader, celebrity, or sports person, and they will describe personal or business success as beginning with a vision, fantasy, or dream which they pursued endlessly. The vision seems remote and impossible at first. By keeping a clear picture in mind and using it to guide their actions and choices, they eventually manifest life-changing results. The actor Jim Carrey famously wrote himself a check for $10 million, adding a note which said, 'for acting services rendered'. He dated it a few years forward, placed it in his wallet, and regularly visualized top Hollywood directors acknowledging and showing interest in his work. He also worked very hard. Carrey used this to keep the faith through difficult career moments. He described the moment when, just before the advance date on the check, he found out he would be earning $10 million dollars on a movie.

For teams to achieve breakthrough performance, we must inspire and motivate them with a vision that captures their imagination. The vision is a detailed picture, not a vague dream or possibility. Goals communicate the steps to fulfilling the vision.

Vision, values, guiding principles, and strategy

Successful companies produce a vision as a frame of reference for the leader and followers; a mental model within which there is an image of a future changed organization, aligned with a future changed environment and an implied or express logic of how to get from here to there. Sometimes values, desired behaviours, and guiding principles complete the picture, all of which are documented in the strategies, plans, and communications. Managers then organize resources around the vision and plan activities to bring it to life.

Shared vision

One global CEO initiated a personal transformation before reinventing the organization. He continually transforms in tandem with the business by creating and engaging the workforce in a vision of the future. A master of the seven powers of transformation, he openly shares reinvention moments with humility and authenticity. At the beginning of a strategy cycle, the CEO works inclusively to develop a vision, which is encapsulated under two or three cornerstone themes. He shares the vision and develops the detailed strategy with a wider leadership group. After visiting many locations to share the message personally, the leadership team follow his lead. Several interventions breathe life into the vision and every opportunity is taken to reinforce messages and clarify links with existing initiatives. The strategy is embedded into leadership development programmes and employee training. Once communicated, the cornerstone themes take on meaning for everyone. Each group adjusts their initiatives and plans to fit the new strategy. Impact is enhanced by:

❖ Telling the story so far. Placing strategic decisions in context and developing pride in company history and progress.

❖ Simplicity of message. Packaging plans under cornerstone themes for digestibility and retention.

❖ A task focused culture. Clear planning and accountability for rapid deployment.

❖ Adaptation of accountability processes and leadership rewards. Motivating leaders to steer in the direction of the strategy. Their behaviour, in turn, influences their teams.

❖ Opinion surveys. Testing implementation by revealing strategy awareness and deployment progress.

> ❖ Companywide communication. Translating the strategy to all employees using different language, media, and frequent updates.
>
> ❖ Conversion of initiatives. Protecting earlier investment and retaining confidence and motivation of employees.

The power of the message

Studies prove that a vision must be radical, demanding, and charismatic to be transformational, and the leader must express and model it passionately. Visions and stories come to life through the power of words, tone of delivery, and body language. The right choice of words create excitement and change a person's state. Words create images and ideas, which trigger emotion in the listener by connecting with their own values, memories, and thoughts. A leader can develop skills in the use of expressive words, sound bites, and theatrical presentation but the communication must inspire, beyond the charisma of the leader.

Chip and Dan Heath in their book *Made to Stick* show how messages have lasting impact when they are simple, unexpected, concrete, credible, and part of an emotional story.[27] With constant competition for our attention, *simplicity* makes a message stick. Find the core of the message and pack meaning into a few words. Frame the vision with a simple headline to make it memorable. 'Ten by Ten' (£10billion revenue by 2010) was the audacious goal of a European business, communicated in a memorable and simple way. Colleagues were able to recall and connect to plans under the 'Ten by Ten' vision and they emulated the brevity of the vision statement in their own plans.

---

[27] Chip and Dan Heath, *Made to Stick: Why Some Ideas Survive and Others Die*, Arrow, 2008.

Our brains are alert to changes or differences; something which is *unexpected*, *surprising*, or off the wall grabs attention. If a red warning light were continuously lit no one would notice. If it flickers with an accompanying bleep, it gets our attention. Break a pattern of behaviour or routine by adding humour where it might not normally exist. Use unusual media or a counterintuitive idea to maintain attention. The following case study is an example of making a vision stick.

A compelling vision

In a logistics business, my HR team and I planned to replace a disparate, outdated, and inefficient HR function with a world-class organization, state-of-the-art systems, and shared services. Still experiencing senior leader resistance after extensive consultation, we decided to bring the plan to life through the medium of television. Senior leaders were invited to a viewing. Inside a company-branded moving vehicle, talking heads popped up in the screen of a navigation system to describe the case for action. The CEO appeared on signposts along the vehicle journey with key messages. An animated service centre and real-life video of familiar faces showcased proposed services. Carefully scripted voice rolled over the unfolding imagery. Leaders watched and listened without interruption. Following a brief discussion, the most cynical leader declared the plan 'a no brainer'. The sentiment resounded and focus turned to the mechanics of moving forward. From that moment on, resistance dissipated, and everyone worked together to overcome obstacles, drive and resource the programme. The movie production process sharpened the vision, removed confusion, and enlivened abstract concepts. The medium of video captured attention in a way that nothing had thus far.

A vision can be abstract because it's about a future that does not yet exist, but it must become *concrete* to mobilize people towards the change. Analogies and metaphors, real-life illustrations, or mini stories make the abstract concrete. Video simulations or vision boards of new processes create images in the minds of an audience struggling to connect. A vision board is a collection of images, symbols, and words representing the vision. By focusing on the board regularly, the mind tunes in and unconsciously scans for possibilities, which move the person towards the vision. When a person connects emotionally with a vision by imagining it happening, how they will feel, and what the outcome will be, the subconscious is programmed. The brain does not know the difference between a real and imagined situation and begins to act as if the vision has already been achieved; responses become automatic. Advertisers take advantage of this phenomenon and carefully design messaging to sink into our subconscious. Athletes use visioning and imagery to improve performance. The athlete conjures an image of their performance; by imagining in a first-person perspective from inside the body or a third-person perspective looking on, they mentally practise their swing or develop their technique. It's more than visualizing; it's a sensory experience of calling to mind physical sensations like muscle tension and rapid heart rate that may be experienced ahead of a performance. From functional MRI studies, we know that visualization and imagery activate motor-processing brain structures,[28] the same neurons we use in physical practice, and this kinaesthetic imagery results in greater activation.

A *credible* vision is believable and underpinned by expertise or authority. Real experience, carefully selected data, and details speak volumes. A well-known expert or authority adds instant

[28] A.J. Adams, 'Seeing is believing: The power of visualization', *Psychology Today*, 3 December 2009. Available from www.psychologytoday.com/gb/blog/flourish/200912/seeing-is-believing-the-power-visualization [accessed 19 May 2022].

credibility. Case studies and examples of success in other organizations make the message believable. To make people care, tap into their *emotion*, and create an association between what they don't care about and something they do care about. During a difficult transformation, the analogy of a 'Tsunami' was used to describe leaders' emotional reactions to minor issues. The offending managers realized the impact of their behaviour, guiltily adjusted their response, and compensated with extra effort.

To make a vision work, people must see what's in it for them. Connect to the self-interest of the audience, and personalize the problem and solution as much as possible. If it's too general, they won't feel compelled to act. When a sceptical and respected CEO addressed top leaders about the benefit of his own personal development, his disarming passion and authentic and vivid delivery was compelling. The group enthusiastically committed to their own plan. Because he cared, they cared.

Stories are more memorable than dry words or lists. Generate a commitment to act by telling the story of the past in a vivid, honest way, and connecting history to the current and future context. A good *story* has a context, a dramatic conflict, formidable challenge, and a resolution. Something magnificent happens, extraordinary results, unexpected relationships, or a creative breakthrough.

Define and refine the vision collaboratively; build ownership and belief. Some people are more passionate than others, but if they understand and believe in the purpose they will perform. A story with a history and a vivid description of the future will mobilize change. The clearer the picture of the outcome, the more detailed the plan and performance, the more likely people will activate it.

The how – goals and objectives

Now imagine in detail the performance and the process or steps leading from the current to future state. I feel I am probably preaching to the converted here; however, for clarity, the vision becomes meaningful and possible through measurable goals. Completed goals provide a sense of progress. They are milestones that signpost and delineate a long journey, a finish line, the shift from the old to the new way of working, and an opportunity for team celebration. Objectives are short-range, accountable tasks, providing the owner with authority to act and a basis for measuring their performance. Goals and objectives must be Specific, Measurable, Achievable, Relevant, and Timed (SMART). Some organizations use OKRs (Objectives, Key Results) or IKOs (Individual Key Objectives) with supporting software to record and track the objective. A strategy is an approach employed to go after the goal, whilst a tactic is a tool, technique or choice used to deliver the objective.

Whilst goals and objectives bring order and productivity, their potential for supercharging motivation is even greater. Studies show that to motivate high performance, we must understand the *importance* and *attainability* of a goal and objective;[29] importance is the driver of commitment, which fuels feelings towards going after the goal. When a person feels the conditions for achievement are positive and supportive, commitment to goals increases feelings of wellbeing, proactive behaviour, and job satisfaction. When a person feels a goal is attainable, they perceive opportunities, control over their work, and are confident of support for achievement. Communication and inclusive development of the vision and shared values contribute to feelings of goal importance and connection. Perception of attainability occurs when we have access to resources, are involved in setting goals and key decisions, and receive leader support,

---

[29] Barbara Steinmann, Hannah P. Klug, and Günter W. Maier, 'The path is the goal: How transformational leaders enhance followers' job attitudes and proactive behavior', *Frontiers in Psychology*, 2018;9: 2338. https://doi.org/10.3389/fpsyg.2018.02338

coaching, nurturing, and confidence building. This can be a very different way of working for task-oriented autocratic leaders who dictate and instruct.

Winning sports teams succeed through a razor-sharp focus on a simple, clear goal and fanatical alignment. In business, goals may exist only in the heads of a few people, or may be woolly, broad, and long term, making it difficult to hold people to account. Long time frames allow procrastination and the growth of distracting priorities. Discussions about success or failure turn into a negotiation over the interpretation or unfairness of work-load. To add to the problem, performance management systems with multi-level ratings encourage 'fence sitting' and mediocrity. Develop crystal-clear simplified goals and objectives, minimize distraction, and avoid overloading people with too many unrelated tasks:

❖ Jointly simplify, tease, and squeeze the goals and objectives for clarity.
❖ Define tangible results and delivery dates.
❖ Implement black and white assessment instead of grading. Goals are either achieved, not achieved, or overachieved.
❖ Remove nice-to-have goals, which dilute focus.
❖ Break large, long-term goals into finite objectives set over daily, monthly, and quarterly time frames.
❖ Agree resources and coaching rhythm. See the 'A' GAME ON approach in Chapter 4.

The plan

The plan is where everything combines: the mission, vision, goals and objectives, and tactics. Simple is better to ensure a focus on what matters. Detailed goals and actions can be captured in a Gantt chart or project planner. The planning process includes charting the goals and objectives, identifying issues, risks, dependencies, and timescales. When the transformation plan is complete, work stream leaders use the same process to plan their priorities with their teams.

Why statement

This is the place to capture purpose, often termed the mission; it's where to show why you do what you do. What are you trying to achieve through your transformation? How will this impact others – customers, organization, industry? As discussed earlier, what is your 'why'?

Vision statement

The vision statement is a short, sharp statement which summarizes the content of your vision (discussed earlier). A handful of words to sum up a vision can be a tough ask. It often takes days of deliberations to find a succinct and meaningful statement. Look beyond simple descriptions of profit or efficiency improvement and dig deep to find the exciting aspects of the vision. If the company needs to become more profitable, what does that really look like? If this is achieved in the next one to three years, what will be happening, what will look and feel different or better?

Goals

The plan contains timed and measured non-financial and financial goals. Break the plan into trackable goal-driven phases and manageable chunks of activity or work streams to make the hefty vision appear achievable. Plan in rewards and a powerful 'surprise' element. The rituals and rewards will be memorable events and team-building opportunities. There are three additional components to the plan.

Where to focus – business/transformation priorities

A business-transforming sales performance needs to know its customers and their needs. Which customers will benefit most from the business offering? Which markets hold untapped potential? Where will we target attention? An internal transformation requires similar answers. Who are the recipients (customers) of the change? What value will be created? Which processes and systems need to transform? A short list of measurable, descriptive goals supported by specific objectives move the team towards the vision, and scarce resources can be diverted into these activities.

How to succeed – success factors/operational priorities

Here we address what needs to be done to implement the new way of working or the service offering to the customer. What are the processes, systems, and operational activities that will deliver the results? Avoid the temptation to list everything that needs improvement; specify activities or systems critical to achievement of the transformation. This may involve living with or reducing focus on some non-urgent operational issues because addressing them distracts from the main goals.

Organizational priorities

Now, we determine the organizational pillars supporting the plan; the people plan, for example, the need to adjust roles and responsibilities of a department, recruit, and train new people. There is a need to update the website, install financial controls, or anything within the organization which needs attention to ensure the smooth running of the transformation. Avoid the temptation to include every organizational problem. Focus only on activities to support transformation. The following case study shows how one business used the planning process to transform.

A plan to perform

XYZ beauty and aesthetics business set a goal to double revenue each year for five years, underpinned by increased average spend per customer, targeted increase in new customers, growth in the 40–60-year-old demographic, product sales, and increased customer satisfaction. The team identified where to focus by segmenting clients. They prioritized focus on the core client demographic and the training of professionals. In determining how to succeed, operational priorities included: the design of exclusive packages targeted at different client groups, development of a unique after-care approach, deployment of a social media strategy, design of learning solutions, and a marketing strategy to draw in practitioners for training. Organizational priorities to transform the business included recruitment of key support personnel, limiting focus on non-revenue generating projects, and relocation of premises.

Measurement and review

Finally, goal power is activated by effective goal tracking and accountability. Progress measurement keeps a project in control, on budget, and highlights the need for course corrections when results are falling behind. It also plays a widely underestimated yet beneficial role in driving motivation, performance, and creativity. Actions are tracked daily; objectives are tracked at weekly or monthly intervals, and goals are usually tracked using monthly and longer-term timeframes. Project management, referenced in Chapter 4, provides the tools for detailing, tracking, and reviewing progress. Accountability processes are explored in Chapter 6.

I recommend automatic, real-time tracking and the use of traffic lights to indicate project status 'at a glance'. Consider fitness trackers used to support personal transformation. The power of these gadgets is real-time data and automatic tracking. They can stimulate physical activity, improved sleep, better eating patterns, and increase the habit of tracking and monitoring. Goal achievement can continually be compared to a target. Once achieved, the user is rewarded with badges, flashing lights, and vibrations. This reward mechanism is not a gimmick; it's carefully designed using gamification, behavioural, and neuroscience insights to leverage intrinsic desires for achievement, status, learning, and socializing. Rewards and their symbols stimulate opioids in the brain which make us happy. Progress updates initiate a burst of dopamine to the brain, creating excitement and curiosity; this activates the brain's seeking system, which drives us to explore new things. Visit transform2outperform.com for a template plan and trackers.

Conclusion

By now, you will understand the need for an inspiring transformational vision and razor-sharp goals and objectives. You also know how to consolidate these into a concise plan which can be measured and tracked to activate goal power. We will now consider the critical processes of transformation and the mechanics of getting things done: process power.

Action points

1.   Find an inspiring shared purpose by understanding who you want to serve and what problems you are solving for them.
2.   When we visualize, we materialize. Build a vivid transformational vision. Use stories to bring it to life;

make it credible, simple, concrete, and make it connect emotionally.

3. Learn from winning sports teams; achieve razor-sharp focus with concise goals, objectives, and tactics. Keep measurement and assessment simple.

4. Connect the dots with an overall plan including a 'why' statement, a vision tag line, financial and non-financial goals, where to focus, how to succeed, and organizational priorities. Limit goals to those crucial to transformation.

5. Measure and review progress constantly to activate goal power.

Chapter 4

Process power

Introduction

A process is a sequence of steps leading to a particular outcome; it can be strategic or transactional. If you are like me, the very word 'process' may incite a desire to eat one's own head! You'll guess, therefore, that following processes and routines is not my natural preference. That said, despite my instincts, I have come to revere the mighty process. Successful transformation and increased efficiency always depend on world-class change management and strict adoption of a well-designed transactional process. We all enjoy freedom to create our own methods, but doing something different every time, whilst exciting, is inefficient. A single intuitive, technology-fuelled, process releases energy from duplicated effort – which can be reinvested in value-creating activities.

In this chapter we tackle the process of ensuring readiness for change. We consider too the strategic change management process; that is, how to effect change collectively and culturally. We drill down into the behavioural, mindset, and capability transformation of teams and individuals, and the more granular change management of operating practices and procedures. We also explore what happens during the change process, the reactions and behaviours faced, and the strategies for handling them.

Change readiness assessment

We learned back in Chapter 1 what can happen when we are not fully committed to, or ready for, change. When the need for change is clear, the temptation is to get on with it. It is vital, however, to make sure the organization and leadership are truly ready.

Resistant or unprepared leadership and inadequate accountability or people management must be addressed before moving forward. During the early design phase, assess and remove derailers before moving on with the plan. Visit transform2outperform.com to see an example readiness checklist.

Culture, leadership, and organization health review

Culture has the power to supercharge or hinder transformation. We therefore need to amplify practices that reinforce new ways of working and remove those that limit progress. We will explore culture power in Chapter 6. Early in the planning it's important to stock take behaviours, styles, and success habits, specifically, those of senior leadership. Successful transformation requires changed habits, practices, and norms; if the leadership, can't accept the need to change behaviour, it's best to stop now. The courage to delay or stop a transformation is as important as the energy to lead it. If the organization is change averse, the top team and culture require attention. A change of people and behaviours at the top of the house is sometimes a prerequisite for transformation, as the following case study illustrates.

Leadership readiness for change

The top leadership of a manufacturing company planned to transform outdated practices to reposition in their market. Engagement surveys and focus groups identified the leaders' operational style. Workshops explored talent strengths, gaps, and the behaviour most recognized and rewarded in the company. The combined results provided a snapshot of culture: a prevalence of autocratic and micromanaging styles considered to be curtailing creativity and engagement; recruitment and promotion practice which reinforced and rewarded controlling behaviours. A restructure, repositioning, and/or replacement of leaders preceded the transformation. The top team refreshed people management policy and practices and implemented a training and career development framework and new leadership reward structure. The business doubled down on accountability quality and cost efficiency. A smooth, companywide transformation occurred; the business withdrew product lines and implemented a new growth strategy.

Explore culture assessment tools which offer the best insights into your business. You may prefer to engage independent help to improve openness and flush out issues. Analyse the following:

❖ Current purpose and identity of the team or organization and ways in which it must differ in the future.
❖ Existing attitudes and beliefs, how they affect performance, which ones need to stay, and which must change.
❖ The processes and practices which reinforce current performance and how they need to change.
❖ Formal or informal reward systems which strengthen personal investment in practices or will help install new practices.
❖ Leadership styles and employee styles or preferences.
❖ Factors supporting/hindering the four core cultural themes of People, Accountability, Customer, and Excellence. See Chapter 6.

Capability assessment

A complex transformation demands crucial capabilities; those of leaders to build the vision, inspire and mobilize the team, and confront the problem; those of the team to adapt to new working methods whilst maintaining service levels to the customer; sufficiency of physical and financial resources; and specialist technical knowledge to support new technology or methods of operation. Map the required capabilities and competence gaps. Source supporting capabilities and check the organization for resilience. See Chapter 8, 'Staying power'.

Critical outcomes

Identify the crux, critical outcomes whereby tackling them means everything else falls into place. Find these during early visioning workouts with stakeholders.

Stakeholder analysis

A stakeholder analysis identifies groups affected by the change, including the people responsible for delivering the change, those impacted directly or indirectly, customers, senior managers, and shareholders. A plan is then formed to consult, communicate, engage, and design solutions which fit their needs.

Spine of influence

Categorize stakeholders as influencers, supporters, or detractors of the programme and maximize the influencers by giving them key roles; eliminate the impact of detractors. See 'During change – influencers, detractors, and toxic behaviour' later in this chapter.

Levels of change

Change management occurs at four levels. The strategic level involves affecting behaviour collectively and culturally on an organization-wide basis. Team change addresses team processes, behaviours, and capabilities. Individual change focuses on individual mindset and beliefs. Operating procedure and process change affects the transactional work of the organization. The value of differentiating the levels is in helping to pinpoint issues and choose strategies to best suit your needs.

Figure 9: Levels of change

Strategic change management

The term 'change management' can confuse; it means influencing groups of people to transform the way they work and setting up the conditions for their success. It's a process of creating a new shared identity, using social influence and collective action to accelerate personal change 'en masse'. Successful transformation is always about the people; when properly supported, they adopt new methods and perform quickly. Consultants may help steer the programme using models and tools or by providing technical expertise to fill resource gaps. The heavy lifting, however, always remains with business teams. The best transformations recruit a blend of part-time and dedicated project resources. These resources are backfilled where possible to minimize disruption to the business. Structures vary according to the nature and complexity of the change. Typically, senior project sponsors steer the programme, whilst a project director coordinates subject matter expert (SME) work streams, led by key personnel.

When we plan the transformation of an organization, we approach the change at the strategic level. It helps to think about three overarching stages:

1. **Visioning the change** – defining and preparing for change, ensuring readiness, and priming the organization for the upheaval. The activities of goal and process power which are explored in this and the previous chapter.
2. **Implementing the change** – the 'nitty gritty' of execution. The activation of people power and culture power to be explored in Chapters 5 and 6.
3. **Reinforcing/sustaining the change** – developing new norms, embedding, and consolidating them in the culture. The capabilities of smart power and staying power to be discussed in Chapters 7 and 8.

John Kotter, Harvard professor and author of *Leading Change*, studied successful change management in many organizations and sets out eight specific steps for successful organizational change.[30] Steps 1 to 3 involve visioning, steps 4 to 6 are implementing steps, whilst steps 7 to 8 involve reinforcing and sustaining the change. The following case study summarizes the transformation of a human resources function in a global business.

---

[30] John Kotter, *Leading Change: An Action Plan from the World's Foremost Expert on Business Leadership*, Harvard Business Review Press, 2012.

A Kotter organizational transformation

The employee/manager experience, costs, and service culture were transformed by removing duplicated labour-intensive work, installing new technology, restructuring, and retraining stakeholders in revolutionized working practices.

Visioning

1. Create a sense of urgency

An education campaign exposed the HR community to external best practice and primed the business for the future vision. Early resistance was countered with examples of inefficiency in current working. Small pilot transformations familiarized the business with change. Executive board members were lobbied on the case for action and the implications of inaction. An external financial crisis provided a burning platform and appetite for change. Once engagement and support strengthened, the vision, business case, and investment were shared.

2. Build a guiding coalition

Each executive board member publicly endorsed the plan and sponsored a feature of the programme, recruiting members of their own teams to provide support and reducing resistance. Key influencers were enlisted in shaping the programme and assigned implementation roles. The appointment of a project director and expert resources proved vital to gaining the confidence of leaders. Work streams comprising people from across the business ensured relevance and a strong connection to business/customer needs.

3. Form a strategic vision and initiatives

The detail behind the high-level vision was compiled over several months, setting out the shape of the new organization, the reorganization, new systems and processes, the description and accountabilities of activities, phasing, and implementation. The flexibility to refine the plan to reflect organizational realities secured the support of the commercial leadership.

Implementing

4.   Enlist a volunteer army

Carefully choreographed communications included: consultation at many levels of the organization about impact on roles and retraining proposals; interactive roadshows sponsored by key leaders to share the vision, road map, preview the new services and training programme, and show empathy and support; work-out sessions to role play new services and discuss the training programme with impacted personnel; roadshow previews to consult with line managers and allow influence over the design and timing of the roll out; customer consultation meetings to communicate and involve them in transition plans; training of new service centre personnel in technical, process, and customer relations skills; training the community to take on business partnering roles. The positive impact ensured 98% of impacted personnel secured rewarding roles in the transformed organization and implementation was fast tracked.

5.   Enable action by removing barriers

As the programme progressed, the vision was enhanced and translated into detailed operating practice. Impacted teams owned the design of the future service, assisted by people with expertise in the new operating model. Frequent challenges and disagreements required a flexible approach and arbitration by senior sponsors. The vision created a movement and momentum; supporters considered it a mandate and quickly turned attention to action. Conflicts were overcome by reliance on vision principles set out early on. Customer-facing teams owned commercial challenges and the solution. Pilot implementations and a price moratorium contributed to customer cooperation. Detractors caused early difficulties and were tackled head on with a strategy appropriate to their complaints. Noise dissipated after successful completion of the first phase.

6. Generate short-term wins

The programme was phased, measured, and celebrated with communications, events, and rewards. Celebration and recognition occurred at phased milestones: achievement of target net promoter scores, new migrations into the service, development of new data-driven capabilities, successful pilot implementations, new service launches and systems launches, and completion of the training programme. More people converted at each milestone and team members grew keen to find roles and invigorate their careers in the new organization.

Reinforcing/sustaining

7. Sustain acceleration

The transformation journey and new capabilities were captured in a story titled 'Fit for growth'. An animated storyboard was used, covering supporter feedback, timeline, achievements, statistics, and a description of the new organization and services for sharing with the stakeholders to develop pride in the team, embed changes in the organization, and support new growth discussions with customers. Training increased understanding and provided the skills for new roles in a new environment. Trainees shared successes, setbacks, and discussed concerns in an informal audience with the executive vice president and project director; issues were redirected to the work streams for resolution. Conversations were used to connect the realities faced by individuals with the vision. The initial pace was cautious; early success led to acceleration, pushing implementation ahead of target. The process and approach were reviewed and refined with strong supporting data and exported into new geographies.

8. Institutionalize change
The removal of former roles and practice forced behaviour change; where roles remained, some defaulted to old practice and adjusted more slowly. General managers were supported through the change. Some adjusted instantly, feeling liberated, whilst others weaned off gradually. Their skill base increased, and they were able to manage without abdicating to a functional colleague.

Team and individual transformation

Sometimes we need to work at the level of the team or individual. Robert Dilts' framework of neurological levels,[31] in conjunction with Kotter's model, is my go-to resource for helping me to analyse issues and decide where to focus for the best result. The model reveals the levels of learning and increased neurological processing that influence the way we experience the world and learn.

> ❖ **Environment** is the *where* and *when* of our lives, where we are faced with opportunities and constraints, get things done, and form relationships. The environment contains influences, which affect minds, which change behaviors, which change outcomes, which change mindset!

---

[31] Robert Dilts, *From Coach to Awakener*, Dilts Strategy Group, 2003, p. 20.

❖ **Behaviours** are *what* we do, the patterns of work, interaction, or communication.

❖ **Capabilities** are *how* we do what we do: the skills, strategies, mental maps, creativity, and decision making we use to get things done.

❖ **Values and beliefs** are *why* we do what we do; they motivate the use of mental strategies and capabilities, support or inhibit behaviours, and affect how we judge and give meaning to our experience.

❖ **Identity** is *who* we are, where the levels combine to create a story about our reality, the type of person we are.

❖ **Spiritual/purpose** is *for whom* or *for what* we do what we do: our perception of the larger systems we feel part of. A sense of meaning directs our actions, capabilities, beliefs, and identity.

The diagram below captures the levels of learning and indicates the direction of change. The target zone for effecting change is across the beliefs and identity levels.

Each level directs interactions at the level below: for example, our identity, the way we see ourselves, affects our beliefs, which affect the capabilities we develop, and so forth. When our identity and beliefs change, everything transforms automatically. It can happen in reverse, although not always, which is often why stuff doesn't appear to work when we change systems and locations at the environment level without attending to beliefs and capabilities. Real change occurs at the belief level. When something contradicts existing beliefs, the mind is forced to consider a new reality; if accepted and reinforced by other experiences, attitude changes, and then capability and behaviour. The levels can help to diagnose blockages and direct action to accelerate change.

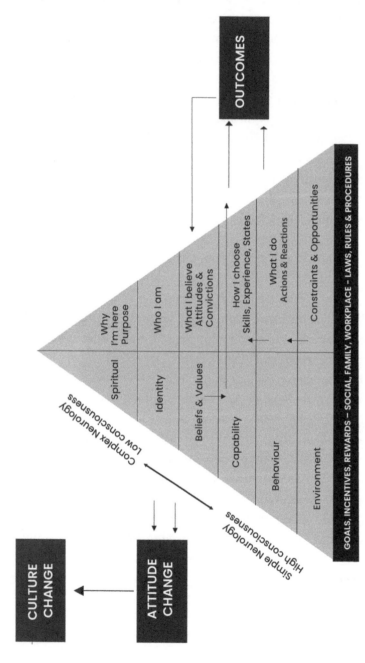

Figure 10: Dilts' neurological levels

Transactional change management

Transforming transactional systems and processes begins in the visioning phase and continues into implementation. This phase reveals the true scale of change. The vision or change solution is analysed for process and system impacts, organizational design consequences, training, engagement, and communication requirements. It is a mistake to focus on the operation or system, presuming that people will follow naturally. Anyone with scars of transformation knows this is not how it works. Job roles that interact with a system or process require redesign, which can affect the basis on which a person is employed. Trained project leaders and process engineers use a range of tools to map and respond to the change.

The process definition phase involves:

- ❖ Impact analysis – the activities to be changed, the nature of impact, the people affected, and the timing.
- ❖ Solution mapping – each process change and associated people impact with milestones and future state definition. People impacts are distinguished in four areas: organization design, skill development, engagement, and communication.
- ❖ Project plan/Gantt chart – a tool which lists detailed tasks, time frames, resource allocation, interdependencies, and conflicts.
- ❖ Review processes – methods of governance, goal tracking, project review, and accountability.
- ❖ Swim lane maps – chart the flow of processes and the touch points between people and technology.
- ❖ Playbook and process design instructions – provides uniform messaging, control, and ownership, accelerating learning and large-scale deployment. The word 'play' implies a user has options. Some playbooks contain mandated instructions and parameters for decision making,

whilst others provide advice on handling people issues or to support changes such as organizational design or a new sales or operational process. Visit transform2outperform. com to download templates.

During change

People love change! It may seem counterintuitive, but we do like change; we relish variety and impose change on ourselves, travelling to new places on vacation, planning exciting activities at the weekend, and changing up our routine at home and work. We enjoy uncertainty and don't like watching the same movie over and over; we become frustrated with repetitive work or constraints that curb our instinct to experiment. The neuroscientist and psychobiologist Jaak Panksepp determined that we have an internal seeking system which must be satisfied and stimulated to be healthy – a strong biological impulse to explore and learn about our environment and derive meaning from what we do.[32] The brain when stimulated releases dopamine, the reward chemical, creating excitement and curiosity. Paradoxically, we also enjoy routine and certainty in some parts of our life, so we develop efficient behaviour patterns which, when disrupted, cause anxiety. For some, work may be the only source of stability in an otherwise chaotic life. Leading change involves reconciling the dilemma of variety and certainty. A good leader works out where certainty and consistency can be maintained and designs the change process to tap into every person's seeking system.

Reactions to change

Initial reactions to imposed change can be negative. When not involved or in control, we may perceive threats to our sense of

---

[32] Jaak Panksepp, 'Affective neuroscience of the emotional BrainMind: Evolutionary perspectives and implications for understanding depression', *Dialogues in Clinical* Neuroscience, 2010;12(4): 533–545. https:// doi.org/10.31887/DCNS.2010.12.4/jpanksepp

competence, personal influence, or livelihood. The uncertainty develops distrust, dissatisfaction, and feelings of injustice. Internal worries build, although they are often not expressed out of fear of being judged. Internal conversation takes over:

'How does this affect me?'

'What's in it for me?'

'How can I protect myself and my interests?'

'How can I continue to look good?'

'Who is influential here and how can I maintain my influence?'

'How can I keep what I have now?'

'What are my team/customers going to think or do?'

'Why is this confusing and unclear? What's their real motive?'

People who actively challenge and question decisions helpfully surface misperceptions and confusion. Managers can mistakenly treat vocal people as troublemakers and shut them down. Apart from the toxic few, these characters are often the most experienced, passionate, and qualified to judge the change. They can also be the most jaded and sceptical, having lived through failed initiatives. The quiet ones may be compliant yet harbour dissatisfaction, form factions, and disrupt in the background. Confusion and clarity are remedied through careful communication, consultation, and involvement. Fears over a lack of competence are allayed through support and training. Trust is built through transparency, including stakeholders in change design, leadership follow-up on commitments, and respectful people management. Support tools ensure consistent people process and personal attention for those impacted.

Involvement, communication, and education

To engage people in transformation, de-activate their natural fear system, involving them ahead of the decision to change and in the process of change. Leaders sometimes restrict information to avoid destabilizing teams. But mystery and intrigue do not inspire. Don't wait until you have all the answers: explain what is and is not available. Otherwise, employees fill in the gaps, imagine Machiavellian motives, and lose trust in their bosses. Employee questions during early consultation help planning and provide useful foresight of issues. Activate the internal seeking system by telling individuals how they fit in, noticing their strengths and putting them to good use. Provide information and choices, letting teams find answers or develop aspects of the programme.

Senior leaders communicate the strategy and risks of not changing, whilst line managers interpret the direct impact on the team, any activities that must change, and the training to achieve this. Leaders of change walk the talk and act out the change they're asking others to make. Their role is to create excitement through two-way dialogue, taking time to reinforce the vision and paint a compelling future. Signposts and hurdles motivate and provide a sense of progress; they are celebration or check points which keep energy high. The use of stories, anecdotes, and metaphors maintain interest and increase memory retention. Real-life stories personalize otherwise dry information, by conjuring pictures in the mind, drawing out emotions, and connecting the unknown with the known. Stories convey subtle or complex information in an understandable way, allowing people to find their own meaning and experience revelations that change beliefs.

Recognition

Leaders must make sure they notice the extraordinary effort required of teams to get transformation done. This can happen in the form of personal feedback, tokens of appreciation, an impromptu or formal celebration event with public recognition and awards, personal development opportunities, or addition of new responsibilities. Whatever the solution, it should occur close enough to the performance and be meaningful.

Coaching

The coaching process is rarely more important than during a difficult transformation. Regular personal contact with a leader during change is affirming and reassuring. Coaching performance at intervals, reviewing goals, discussing progress, delivering feedback, agreeing alternatives, and choosing actions maintains accountability and drives high performance. It can be demanding of a leader's time, but a skilled coach steers succinct goal-focused conversations in a short, powerful session. Different people and contexts demand interpersonal skill and judgement. I use my 'A' GAME ON approach to develop coaching skills.

Figure 11: 'A' GAME ON approach

Authenticity

A coaching relationship is built on rapport; the feeling of congruence, authenticity, and safety built early in the engagement. Rapport simplifies communication, eliminates resistance, and heightens coach credibility. It often happens automatically when we like someone. To relax a person and increase connection, try subtly matching and mirroring their physiology; pace the volume, tempo, and modulation of your voice; and select terminology which fits their view of the world. Encourage the learner to ask questions and raise concerns so they get used to the two-way nature of the process. Make sure they understand their responsibility for performance optimization and seek their consent to be coached. To increase receptiveness to feedback and accelerate the shift to concise and productive goal discussions, focus early on strengths – analyse where they show up, what triggers them, and how they can be applied further. The coaching relationship is sensitive and can involve unravelling entrenched beliefs, behaviours, and vulnerabilities. An experienced coach may selectively share an aspect of their own vulnerability to remove barriers and empathize with a learner's experience.

Goals

Performance goals or tasks are the primary focus of a dynamic coaching session. Encourage self-reflection by asking open questions about goals, challenges, and feelings. Lead the person to assess the context in which they do and do not experience performance difficulties, how they create their problem performance, what goes through their mind, and what internal conversation they have at the time. Teach them to be concise. The listening process helps the person develop their own insight into their performance or problem. The coach speaks only to question or direct the learner, taking notes highlighting points for later discussion. Ask the learner to decide whether a goal has been achieved with a firm yes or no answer, taking care not to agree or disagree at this stage.

Active listening

Discipline yourself to listen and capture information: 'Tell me more', 'What happened next?', 'What else?', 'Why?'. Crucial points are missed when the mind is focused on preconceptions or a desire to interrupt. Go beyond active to *extreme* listening, using one-word questions to elicit information until the individual has no more to give. The answers to how, why, and what questions provide clues to supporting them. People reveal more and deeper levels of information when faced with an open question and long silence. The experience of being heard is therapeutic and empowering. The data captured provides the coach with the language of the learner's world and hints at the direction of the solution.

Mirror

At the appropriate moment, add value by selecting insights, para-phrasing, and playing back information reflecting the descriptive words used by the person. 'So, what I have heard you say is...' This mirror process reframes their input, demonstrates that they have been heard, allows them to hear their feedback outside of their own head, diffuses emotional connection to the information, and stimulates further reflection. Performance, goal achievement, and development are summarized through this iterative process of mirroring input and calibrating understanding. Be sure not to label the person, e.g. 'You're not good with targets'. Words have power and, in certain contexts, labels become negative beliefs which cause problems later.

Experience

Add your experience by homing in on features of performance, analysing success, or providing performance improvement advice. The learner usually responds openly after a focus on strengths. Weave your own perspective in with the learners to make the switch between strong performance results and improvement opportunities flow naturally. When a positive climate has been created, the coach (and respondent) must be prepared to enter a zone of uncomfortable debate, when necessary, to motivate change. The more frequent the conversations, the more dynamic and easier it becomes to 'cut to the chase', taking care to avoid complacency.

Options

Explore possibilities for fine tuning. Analyse parts of performance, visualizing a new outcome, and calculating the resources, conditions, and skills needed to get there. The learner metabolizes the change more fully when they own their solution. The change comes from within. This is a natural result of a successful coaching conversation. If the learner is overwhelmed and fails to see the route through, the coach is more directive, pushing the individual to specific choices or alternatives. If performance is strong, the coach works with the learner to find marginal performance gains and seek greater challenge and complexity. If the performance gap is wide, prioritize the steps to performance improvement and provide closer support through those steps.

Next steps

Unless there's firm commitment to time-definite and measurable next steps, nothing happens. This crucial step is easily missed in the weight of general discussion. The engagement must end with a next step and a simple, realistic, and practical plan for action. If the plan is complex, it is not a coaching plan. The behaviour and performance must be chunked into small components to make change achievable, allowing new habit formation and early feelings of success.

Handling resistance

Resistance is mostly a natural behaviour, caused by the grieving process that people experience during change. See Figure 12 below. With good communication and involvement, many can move swiftly from the old to the new, whilst others feel the change more deeply. First comes shock, disbelief, and a performance dip caused by the anxiety. This progresses to a state of denial and inaction as the person seeks to reinforce the status quo; a period of frustration with a sense of unfairness and the development of resistance behaviours. An unsuccessful fightback leads to a stage of depression and discomfort. In time, the person moves to exploration, acceptance, commitment, and renewed performance. Those that fail to overcome their grief tend to leave or, worse, remain in the organization embittered and resentful. The leader's task is to help individuals move quickly through the curve and prevent the despair that causes talent to give up and move on. Communication and involvement at an early stage prevent anxiety and move people quickly to acceptance and performance. Some will need more support for differing reasons.

Anticipate the grief process and warn people of these feelings to reduce feelings of isolation.

- ❖ Begin dialogue; acknowledge, empathize, and legitimize the feelings and listen for resistance reasons.
- ❖ Offer solutions, trials, and explanations to accelerate acceptance.
- ❖ Find new ways to energize them towards the future.

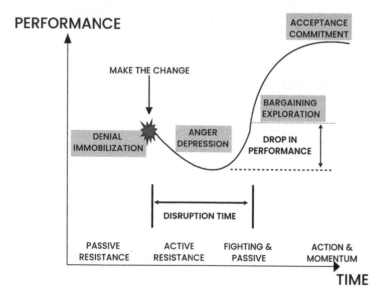

Figure 12: Reactions to change

Influencers, detractors, and toxic behaviour

People that bypass the grief curve generally become influencers; they can rationalize the plan and become passionate supporters, helping to transform at pace. Those that get stuck in the negative feelings become detractors as they go in search of support for their point of view and damage productivity. Understanding these behaviour types and addressing them keeps the programme on track. People facing change fall into five archetypes: Super Players, Players, Tourists, Prisoners, and Escaped Prisoners.

Super Players are characterized by high influence and high engagement. They aren't always senior people; they may be experts or long-serving employees with a good reputation. Super players get on board, drive the change, and engage others. They can be instrumental in converting the attitudes of others and maintaining momentum. These key change agents should be identified early and given leading roles in the programme.

Figure 13: Behavioural types during change

Thankfully most people quickly become **Players**, the early adopters who get involved. They may not own the plan like a super player, but they embrace the plan and get stuff done. Players should be enlisted to influence others and buddy with a tourist or a prisoner. They should have a key role in the programme and be rewarded and recognized for successes.

Tourists are casual observers, perhaps not initially impacted by the change or slightly sceptical. They get on with life as they know it and wait to see how things turn out. Some tourists convert quickly into players or join in once they've seen how the cards are dealt. They can become prisoners if they miss the boat by staying out of the fray. Telling tourists you notice them 'sitting on the fence' can increase their engagement or expose the reason they're hedging their bets. Focus on influential tourists: when they move, others follow.

Prisoners, usually fewer in number, are active resistors, locked in the old world and their own perspective. The communication and work to alter mindset have had little impact on these people. They create doom and gloom, rally others for support, sabotage efforts, and create political barriers. Listen carefully to their objections and address them; restate why change is necessary. If you've failed to overcome issues, block their ability to resist or not comply if possible. If they still don't want to engage, point out the consequences. If they persist, their presence is damaging and they should be moved on respectfully. Leaders can be reluctant to act on prisoners because of their valued skill set or experience. But when there is no hope of conversion, delay damages confidence in the programme. Whilst some seem inconvertible, there are occasions when, after witnessing success, the most strident prisoners experience a mindset change and become fanatical supporters of the new order.

The most dangerous of all are a small group of **Escaped Prisoners** who typically hold senior roles. Keep an eye out for escaped prisoners; hints are in their communication and personal status motives. They appear to go along with the change and masquerade as super players. Escaped prisoners wait for their moment and act to turn back the clock, revert to old practice, and become the hero amongst other prisoners. They enjoy their hero status, use drama and extremes to persuade others and warn of exaggerated consequences, in the interests of being right or getting their own way. Explore the real evidence behind their emotionally fuelled assertions and they are less plausible than they first sound. Flush them out where possible and point out discrepancies between what they say and do. Access the people who can influence them. Call out and question their intentions to get them signed up on the record.[33]

---

[33] Note: I first heard someone use the terms Prisoner, Tourist, and Player in a presentation and have been unable to locate a source of these archetype names. I adopted these names, added definitions, along with the Super Player and Escaped Prisoner archetypes and the strategies for responding.

Toxic leaders

A positive leadership attitude is vital because they influence the mindset of so many people. Transformation, however, can bring out the best and worst in people. Some leaders become super players and others prisoners. Their insecurity and dwindling sense of power exacerbate behaviours and create a toxic environment. Apart from those with diagnosed personality disorders, people are generally not toxic: the outcome of their behaviour is. They are passionate people, largely well intended and often not aware of the effect they have on others; it's quite possible that in other areas of their work and life they impact positively. Leaders who create toxicity are bullies because of the stressful impact their words and behaviours have on their teams.

Toxic team behaviour

All of us are capable of a toxic moment but it's not our normal style. Some people display these behaviours more consistently: they are political, insecure, ambitious, and seek to increase their own influence or reduce that of others.

Team members who create toxicity undermine a programme and team performance with their negativity and disloyalty.

Addressing toxicity

Toxic behaviour can be subtle and difficult to pinpoint but must be tackled before the rot sets in. The following steps suggest an approach to addressing toxicity.

1. Decipher toxic behaviours that you witness in your team or other teams. Use the list of toxic types at transform2outperform.com or produce your own list. Describe the behaviour you see and the apparent intention of the behaviour. Describe the impact on others; identify

triggers of behaviour and likely causes. Give the behaviour an archetype name.

- Archetype
- The trigger
- The behaviour
- Impact on others
- The intention (positive and negative)

2. Scrutinize your own behaviour for signs of toxicity. You are unlikely to perceive your impact as toxic; such effects are mostly experienced by others, but under close examination you may find hints. Have you experienced a surprising reaction from a person or received personal feedback? Are people open or guarded with you? Encourage people to give you feedback one to one. If you are uncomfortable applying this within the team you lead, seek input from a peer or trusted colleague. Ask about your positive and less positive impacts.

3. Work with a team to describe 'red card' behaviours and train everyone in their impact. Call out possible bad behaviours ahead of change to encourage self-reflection. Use a yellow card process to allow the team to signal bad behaviour when they see it.

4. Train people to give feedback. No one should be labelled toxic; it's the impact of behaviour that is toxic and only upon those who perceive it that way. Assertive feedback means describing a behaviour and its impact on the *feelings* of others, taking care not to personalize it, showing empathy for the behaviour and asking for a remedy which works for everyone. Imagine receiving this feedback. 'When you criticize my performance in the team meeting, I *feel* hurt and humiliated. I *appreciate* that you need to

raise concerns; *can we agree* an approach to addressing these privately with me, improving my ability to respond?' The recipient knows what behaviour is causing a problem; the (bad) behaviour is not judged, but the impact is. Even people who appear consistently toxic don't enjoy being responsible for the distress of others; they often do not realize their impact and react by overcompensating.

5. During team-building events, work through toxic archetypes in a fun way. Explore behaviours and their causes. Ask the team to identify other toxic impact; they often enjoy creating new archetypes. The process helps individuals to recognize their own tendencies, understand the feelings and motivations driving them, and make better choices.

Tackling the toxic boss and team members

Tackling a toxic boss can be tough. Bosses tend to feel their behaviour is good performance management, passion, or appropriate leader behaviour. You may need to check whether you are reacting emotionally or over-interpreting their behaviour. When convinced of the problem, consult trusted colleagues or a mentor and/or work with a human resources colleague. An assertive response, delicately prepared, is important; be prepared to deal with what might occur. Most people are initially defensive and then later adopt the feedback, trying to correct their behaviour. In the worst cases their behaviour may intensify. The options at this point are to seek organizational help, work with a supportive mentor in the background, or choose to redeploy out of the untenable relationship.

Authentic leaders and team members who are comfortable with their strengths and weaknesses tend to create a positive climate. The minority who cause a toxic environment with hostile and emotional behaviour, judgement, critique, and complaint require early attention to prevent distractions and relationship problems.

Conclusion

High-quality processes which support people affected by or implementing change help build a great people culture. Post transformation, the organization is more agile and employee friendly. The standards of communication, consultation, and engagement create a new expectation, which must be sustained to keep the organization and the team change ready.

This chapter concludes the visioning and preparation phases of transformation. It's time to focus on making it happen through people power and culture power.

Action points

1. Resource a dedicated project team, people with capabilities who can be seconded part time and resources to backfill any gaps created.
2. Assess culture, leadership, organizational health, and team readiness for change before proceeding.
3. Assess the team. Create a plan using Dilts' neurological levels to work on achieving mindset change.
4. Organize change activities under visioning, implementation, and reinforcement. Cross-reference Kotter's change model to make sure the lessons are incorporated in plans.
5. Analyse the impact of change. Map out the process/system change milestones and corresponding change to organizational design, job definition, skill development, engagement, and communications.
6. Identify influencers and detractors; work out their role in the programme and strategies for converting people into players and super players.
7. Develop supportive people processes to accompany change, and pre-handle toxicity.

Chapter 5

People power

Introduction

Organizations don't transform; people do. An organization is merely a legal document and a plan that exists only in the imagination of the founder. The magic happens when people come together to build buildings and technology, imagine ideas, and create or change products and services. The organization and transformation come to life through people power, the exceptional value, performance, and reputation that come about when teams develop and use their combined strengths.

In this chapter we consider how to resource a team for transformation, how to set up the conditions for their success, and how to build competence. We look at the importance of matching people to the right roles, getting the team in shape, dealing with early performance issues, and embedding sticky learning into the transformation process. Crucially, we explore how to engage the team through the creation of an extraordinary experience, including a detailed look at mental health and wellness. Finally, we find how to boost people power through the creation of a high-performing symbiotic team.

A team to transform and outperform

Spot talent

People power begins with matching the right personalities, strengths, and motivation to the task. To transform we must see the team through fresh eyes. It's time to mix it up a little, examine attitudes and skills, as if people are joining the business for the first time. Use old skills in new ways to re-energize and rejuvenate.

Take a technical specialist out of their comfort zone; let them use their organizing skills or work in a new field. Appoint the best people to critical tasks. These personalities shape the programme, challenge the status quo, and are great communicators. They are respectful, change oriented, able to produce results in unchartered situations. They navigate and work the organization, and engage support. Importantly, they don't create drama, sweat the small stuff, or become easily offended. The worst candidate is the emotional drain who sees insult at every turn, defends their power base, and believes everything they tell themself. Ask them to ditch the drama; alternatively, redeploy them to alternative roles or they will limit innovation and create friction.

Look for people who show evidence of:

- technical expertise and a unique application of these skills;
- skills critical to the transformation and business;
- analysis, creativity, and judgement in solving problems;
- flexibility and openness to alternatives;
- empathy, self-awareness, and influential communication;
- high motivation and mental resilience;
- experience of thriving in similar transformations.

Source critical experience

Resource proven experience to help formulate the vision and build credibility with stakeholders. An experienced professional is more plausible, clear, and convincing than a well-intentioned amateur. Whilst it's good to assign team members to different roles, it's dangerous to allow mission-critical skills to be developed on the fly. Critical skills can be recruited or seconded into the team or subcontracted from specialist teams and consultancies who can leave expertise behind when they move on. New roles and consultants create tensions because these change agents tend to gain a strong power base, whilst the existing team see their influence erode. Invest in rebuilding the newly formed team; focus on mindset and adjusting to a new reality. Reduce anxiety and improve feelings of significance by making room for everyone to own part of the plan.

Assess culture fit

Ensure a person can adapt to the values and collective behaviours of the team or organization. Consider cultural fit from two angles: the ability of the individual to fit the team and the ability of the team and culture to adapt to an individual. This is key when they bring a missing skill set or when there's a need to modify culture. Poor fit is deeply uncomfortable and unproductive. To assess fit, meet the person in a range of settings. Arrange for them to meet several people informally. Use evaluation tools and structured interviews to explore personality, styles, values, and motivators. Explore what frustrates them, makes them happiest, motivates them and is important to them, in life and at work. Understand how they handle conflict and feedback, and how they work within and lead a team.

Attract diversity

Diverse thinking styles and experience are invaluable for transformation. Different experts, customers, and other stakeholders are important allies in solving problems and are well placed to connect the new with the old, or to spot hidden land mines. If accustomed to working in a homogeneous team, exposure to diversity can be a shock to the system. Progress seems slow and opinions are difficult to reconcile. With patience, immense benefits result from collaborating with different types of people, whether in terms of nationality, gender, race, age, expertise level, industry, or company experience. When I started working internationally, my brain had to work harder to view the world through the cultural lens of my colleagues. It was a small price to pay for the improved quality of solution that always transpired. From that moment on, working without the interest and rewards of diversity felt limiting and unappealing.

The power of diversity

When transforming two large international businesses into one global powerhouse, success lay in combining respective leadership strengths to create a single high-performance culture. Working with Fons Trompenaars, author and culture expert, we surveyed the leadership and identified strong results focus, the financial excellence and process focus of one culture and the innovation, experimental, and entrepreneurial approach of the other. The steps to successful transformation included:

❖ Understanding – getting to know each group through a structured approach to sharing business knowledge, processes, and tools.
❖ Appreciating differences – developing respect for the capabilities of the two teams through communication and joint integration planning.
❖ Reconciling differences and critical competencies to create new value – selecting the best leadership group and adopting the best tools and processes from either business.
❖ Balancing the leadership – selecting and retraining internationally diverse leaders.

The business transformed into a disciplined, entrepreneurial business, more inclined to explore alternative markets and interests with strong financial guardianship, rigorous process deployment, and innovation. The diversity offered greater competence, imagination, confidence, and expertise in new markets and the business outperformed market expectations.

Recruit a diverse team. Seek out dynamic talent of diverse cultural and business backgrounds with a drive to succeed and deliver, a people focus, and a blend of expertise and transformation leadership ability. Avoid recruiting people less talented than yourself. Find those whose talent you believe can surpass your own. You are judged as a leader on the performance and talent of your team, not the extent to which you must intervene to fill the competence gap. A manager recruiting in their own image or less limits the potential of scarce resources. Finding partners and colleagues who complement rather than copy increases power.

Establish a team identity

We are all tribal in nature; we favour our own group over others and declare our own group 'us' and other groups 'them'. Even the most introverted person benefits from connecting with others; it's a question of survival. Teams who work in dangerous circumstances, military teams in war zones, fire service workers, mineworkers, and police officers, face perilous situations yet continue to step in harm's way. The shared meaning, facing the unknown, and the significance of serving others builds alliances, memories, and lifelong bonds. In crisis situations they seem able to combine strengths to demonstrate higher levels of capability, courage, and commitment. Help the team to understand their strengths, trust, and care for each other by working together on tasks, having fun, and sharing personal vulnerability.

Build competence

A transformation calls for new technical, process, and behavioural skills. The definition of new competencies involves working with teams, leaders, and experts to flush out the gap in existing skills, knowledge, and experience. The change may require minor adjustment of tools, addition of new competencies or, in the case of a companywide transformation, a new or refreshed competence framework. Competencies depend on the needs of the job and the culture of the company. It takes time and research to build a framework with some organizations preferring a scientific approach. In today's fast-paced environment, a shortlist of competencies intensively developed with flexibility to accommodate future changes is popular. My SPACE system (see Chapter 6 on culture power) is based on five core competency descriptors, which can be adjusted, tailored, and behaviourally anchored for different career levels within an organization (see the following table). Focus on a tight set of competencies to keep things simple and accelerate change. Design a supporting career path and training solutions and choreograph the change programme to maximize learning and deepen competence.

Style	Being self-aware, open, authentic, and values driven. Building a strategic vision and leadership brand. Leading change with presence, humility, and emotional intelligence. Staying abreast of technical, professional, and leadership trends. Sharing knowledge and expertise. Inspiring others to become expert.
People	Creating a vibrant, collaborative environment where diverse teams flourish. Engaging teams with empathy, coaching, training, and respectful communication.
Accountability	Driving and owning results. Using accountable processes, behaviours, and measures. Creating openness, constructive performance dialogue, and respectful performance coaching.
Customer	Connecting with consultative, transparent commercial relationships. Providing value and positive experience through innovation, market/industry expertise, cost focus, product, and service excellence.

Excellence	Pursuing best-in-class standards and results. Sponsoring continual improvement. Building a reputation for completing and finishing.

Table 1: SPACE competencies

Deploy to strengths

As mentioned in Chapter 2, noticing a person's strengths and putting them to good use makes them happier, and more energized and productive. They spend less time focusing on weaknesses or getting bent out of shape to fit in, and more time on mastering skills and getting results. The matching process involves defining the job, and assessing personality strengths, technical and interpersonal skills, performance levels, and other attributes. In common practice, role definition is sketchy, personal strengths are ignored, and the flexibility to design work around a person's strengths is limited by the culture of an organization; however, there are massive performance gains to be had. Help the team to find and elevate their strengths.

Dynamic team 360

My preferred tool for developing team strengths is a dynamic 360-degree speed dating, a live process with instant impact. The process builds respect, reduces tension, solves relationship issues, improves team performance, and works well with all teams, including senior executives who rarely receive unfiltered personal feedback. In a dynamic process, the whole team and their manager participate simultaneously. Each person completes feedback ahead of a 'speed dating' exercise. For each colleague and team manager, the simple survey includes:

❖   a shortlist of evaluation questions to score along a scale;

❖ a description of three colleague strengths that contribute to team performance, with supporting examples;

❖ a description of one opportunity to improve contribution.

The scores are aggregated anonymously for each colleague. Strengths and improvement opportunities are collated so that each person receives a compilation, identified by the colleague providing the feedback, which is shared before the event. At the speed dating exercise, each team member engages in a time-limited interaction to discuss the feedback with their date. One person gives feedback and the other receives it, swapping roles at half time. All feedback begins with strengths. Following the speed dating exercise, each team member commits to one theme to enhance performance, building on their strengths. The follow-up process is agreed, and progress is discussed at intervals.

The benefits of the process are:

❖ The person writing feedback takes care as they own the message in face-to-face follow-up.

❖ Examples increase relevance and quality of feedback.

❖ The strengths focus drives a positive atmosphere.

❖ The team is open to improvement opportunities after a focus on strengths.

❖ Strengths are reinforced through repeated evidence from different colleagues.

❖ There is little delay between completing the survey and sharing the results.

❖ Accountability for performance is increased and relationships improve.

Development dashboard

Combining data from a variety of assessments in a development plan and dashboard builds confidence and performance when jointly validated by the individual and their boss. With consistent leadership follow-up, performance improves and the culture changes. In transformational situations, assessments provide a snapshot of talent and potential. The organization's standard tools can be integrated with new tools to suit specific needs. In one organizational integration, tools to measure conflict handling styles, leadership styles, verbal and numerical reasoning, and career preferences were compared with performance data and used to match individuals to roles and succession plans. In another, tools to assess leadership style, the climate created by leaders, competencies, communication styles, and potential assessments informed a culture change. Participants benefitted from a personal dashboard integrating the results, professional coaching support to interpret and validate results, manager validation, and career planning. The greatest performance gain occurred when managers consistently committed to the support and validation of their team members and sustained follow-up effort.

Career planning

Career planning increases the likelihood of an individual matching a targeted role. In one organization, a simple process became one of the most respected tools used to match talent to key roles and develop strengths.

The six overarching steps are:

- ❖ **Identification** of strengths, ambitions, career preference, experience, and skills through interview and data review.
- ❖ **Validation** of strengths and preferences by the manager.
- ❖ **Options** are discussed with the manager. Specific roles and types of roles are explored. One or two viable role options are mapped as likely career steps and a role option is targeted one step beyond the next role.

- ❖ **Competence** is determined to qualify for next roles, including the skills, behaviours, and experience necessary to achieve best fit.
- ❖ **End goals** are identified as four broad development goals which build on strengths and develop experience leading to the target roles.
- ❖ **Specific actions and experiences** are devised to meet the goals.

When the plan is complete, the manager and plan holder are tuned in to opportunities and ensure the employee moves towards filling the specified roles.

Deal with poor fit or performance

Inevitably, a team in transformation face a changed set of duties, processes, and working environment. Hopefully, communication and involvement interventions have inspired the desire to adapt. The right communication helps people to self-select into or out of the future. There are always individuals who don't want to fit into the new world, are too invested in the way things are currently done, or are fearful of change. If fit remains poor after working through issues, divert or redeploy people quickly. When handled elegantly, these situations set a tone of trust for the programme and prevent a climate of fear or negativity. Redeployment strategies or respectful exit solutions are created during the planning stage. Through training and coaching most people adjust to the new environment and are engaged by new technology or a feature of the role which makes life easier. Three months is sufficient to determine fit, although achievement of an individual's peak performance is unlikely during this time. Steps can be taken to prevent poor performance during the early stages.

The ABCDE of dealing with poor fit or performance

Accountability

Agree accountabilities and a method of holding the team accountable, a two-way dialogue concerned with determining standards and the mechanisms for addressing failure. An inclusive approach to accountability increases commitment to work within the agreed parameters. The leader must also be willing to be held accountable.

Figure 14: ABCDE of dealing with poor fit

Behaviours

Work together on desirable behaviour and culture to ensure the team model the change. Agree a charter of behaviours, a transparent and non-threatening process for calling out positive or unhelpful actions or behaviours to help the team adjust. One team I know use a yellow card to be raised when someone sees unhelpful behaviour. The group strike a healthy balance between serious and light-hearted reproach, keeping the atmosphere pleasant and productive.

Crucial conversation

A crucial conversation is defined by Kerry Patterson, Joseph Grenny, Ron McMillan, and Al Switzler in their book *Crucial Conversations* as a conversation of opposing opinions, where the stakes are high and emotions charged.[34] Many of us face them at different times in our life and career and sometimes handle them badly. A conflict or difficult issue should be tackled early; stalling is harmful for everyone. These conversations create a new level of trust, regardless of the outcome. The simplest strategy for tackling crucial conversations is the assertive response: describe in detail the issue or event, explain current feelings and the impact on you and others, describe your idea of what you want, hold dialogue, listen hard, and seek suitable compromise.

Dynamic coaching

Dynamic observation and coaching during the first three months help a new person settle in and support an existing team member through change. See the 'A' GAME ON approach in Chapter 4. To be dynamic, it must be frequent, simple, and flexible. To be coaching it must be a dialogue, not a one-way conversation. Short, sharp informal discussions that focus on one aspect of the day, the performance, or the behaviour keep the focus high and intensity light. Occasional coaching moments which acknowledge or

---

[34] Kerry Patterson, Joseph Grenny, Ron McMillan, and Al Switzler, *Crucial Conversations: Tools for Talking When Stakes Are High*, McGraw Hill, 2011.

support milestones of progress and performance boost morale and discretionary effort.

Ending with dignity

If there is no resolution after crucial conversations and reviews, plan a redeployment. Carefully screen conclusions of poor fit for discrimination and unconscious bias. Regardless of the outcome, the role or task should end with the sense of a continuing relationship where possible and an individual's contributions honoured.

Design sticky learning

Transformation is the business of changing minds, which means communicate, train, and pump as much information into the brain as possible, right? Wrong! Learning and change happen when we try to get knowledge *out* of the brain when we process, engage, interact with, and re-frame experiences. We have known for some time, courtesy of David A. Kolb,[35] that we learn in a cycle of experience, reflective observation, theorizing, and experimentation. The goal, therefore, is to increase *processing, speed, and scale of learning* by driving the team through the complete cognitive cycle during the design and implementation of transformation and using technology and resources in new and exciting ways.

❖ Plan specific work experiences for learning.
❖ Shape supporting communication and information to allow time for reflective thinking.
❖ Involve people in the decisions, ideas, and solutions.
❖ Let them experiment.

---

[35] David A. Kolb, *Experiential Learning: Experience as the Source of Learning and Development*, Prentice Hall, 1984.

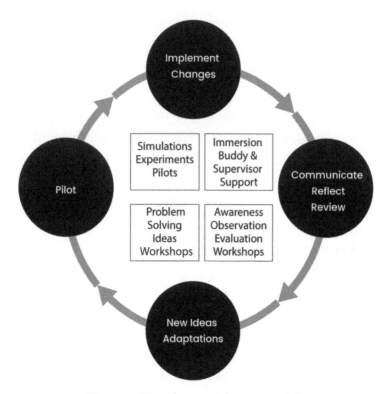

Figure 15: Transformation learning cycle[36]

Awareness

Introduction to transformation is best suited to workshops or conferences. The purpose is to communicate the context, vision, business case for action, and benefits. People decide their personal position: 'I'm in', 'I'm out' or 'I'm on the fence'. Face-to-face contact and two-way dialogue is key for checking the temperature and responding quickly to detractors. Typical outcomes at this stage include:

- ❖ buy in to rationale for change;
- ❖ confidence in the programme, its leaders and teams;
- ❖ identification of issues or gaps in the plan;

---

[36] Adapted from and based on Kolb's Learning Cycle.

* engagement and accountability for action;
* awareness of immediate processes;
* establishment of two-way dialogue;
* early input of colleagues to the detailed vision.

Sessions should ensure uncomplicated and digestible information. Team discussion allows processing of new information, sharing of perspectives, and constructive challenge. Interactive technology and anonymous voting systems gauge opinions and concerns. Online solutions and video are effective, although no substitute for the connection and collaboration of face-to-face engagement. By using these events to involve people in building the detailed vision, we force them to introspect and rationalize abstract ideas and make plans to pilot changes.

Immersion

We master skills and intensify learning through immersion and real experience. Team leaders can do a few simple things to increase the learning from real-life experience.

* Design in reflection sessions – time to think, opportunities to discuss experience with others, exploration of new ideas.
* Increase supervised learning – manager observations and immediate one-to-one feedback.
* Plan intense practice for activities which occur infrequently; use simulations to increase understanding and recall.
* Use the flipped classroom, explained below – make classroom learning available at home, and use valuable workshop time to develop practical skills.
* Elevate the learning experience – make it a peak moment filled with pride and connection.
* Appoint a training buddy – cultivating subject matter experts as trainers grows transformation capability.

Coffee and sticky bytes

We live in an infobesity crisis; ubiquitous information competes for our attention. Who hasn't allowed precious time to be swallowed up by a headline or clickbait? If, like mine, your brain works like a sieve on steroids, you may be frustrated by an inability to recall material. According to neuroscientist Adam Gazzaley, author of *The Distracted Mind*, our ability to perceive or recall data and use it to make choices depends on the brain being able to filter relevant information.[37] The more irrelevant the data bombarding us, the more difficult it is to retain what matters. Carefully select information and interactive training to steer a team through short stimulating learning during a brief work pause. Bite-sized learning interwoven within the workday increases capacity for retention by providing the variety that the brain enjoys. See in the following example how one manager met the challenge.

Learning cafe

A busy operations manager worked with her teams to design two unique learning cafe locations. Each conveyed a different personality through attractive and tranquil design, a stark contrast to an industrial operation. Technology was installed and teams visited the location at different times of the day for group and individual learning bytes. The learning material was developed with the help of specialists, although teams were regularly assigned to develop content to educate other teams. The site operated a daily pulse check survey, which reported increased positive engagement response – notably, increased perceptions of organizational interest in their development and opportunity to progress.

---

[37] Adam Gazzaley and Larry D. Rozen, *The Distracted Mind: Ancient Brains in a High-Tech World*, MIT Press, 2016, pp. 59–94.

Professors Robert and Elizabeth Bjork at the University of California pioneered the idea of 'desirable difficulties' in learning.[38] A learner must endure a feeling of frustration during learning, which leads the brain to process material more deeply and creates longer-lasting memories, much like the feeling of resistance during physical exercise improves long-term results. To be desirable, the challenge or difficulty must be something a learner can overcome through increased effort. To design learning experiences that offer challenge and greater cognitive processing:

- ❖ Use challenging questions and a pre-test to explore knowledge before the session – this primes the brain to absorb the correct information later and increases retention by 10–15% over passive learning.
- ❖ Engage the team in passing on knowledge by designing their own learning bytes. Testing yourself on what you've learned is called 'retrieval practice' and is one of the most reliable ways of building memory. The more difficult the retrieval, the stronger the long-term learning.
- ❖ Limit time on one topic. Bite-size learning naturally achieves this. Moving on to other activities or topics causes momentary frustration, which increases long-term recall.
- ❖ Time the learning after active physical exertion, even if this is just moving to a new location. The physical activity triggers the release of neurotransmitters essential for memory formation.
- ❖ Schedule the learning to take place in different places. Learning is context dependent and may be blocked in different situations unless agility is created through exposure to a new context.

---

[38] Robert R.A. Bjork and Elizabeth L. Bjork, 'Desirable difficulties in theory and practice', *Journal of Applied Research in Memory and Cognition*, 2020, 9(4): 475–479. https://doi.org/10.1016/j.jarmac.2020.09.003

❖ Allow a relaxing coffee pause or two in a quiet place to allow learning to take hold whilst the unconscious brain does its work.

The flipped classroom

The flipped classroom involves exchanging the traditional 'class lecture then homework' with a home study lecture followed by a discuss and develop in class approach. The learner is routed to carefully designed learning activity before coming to a meeting or event. The event or meeting focuses on practical application of the learning, group work, or answering questions. Delegates attend with a level knowledge base and can engage in discussion, simulation, and collaborative work. The key differences between flipped classroom and the traditional approach are that:

❖ the coach provides access to the lesson using pre-recorded video and pre-prepared slides, animation, or other engaging content;
❖ offline lessons are designed to foster curiosity, engagement, and interaction;
❖ delegates can access the lessons repeatedly or in bite-size pieces for convenience and understanding;
❖ face-to-face sessions are used for practising skills, collaborative work, and deeper discussion.

Technology and structuring content

Tools like Thinkific and Teachable are widely used online presentation and learning tools for adults. Many companies have a learning management system that can host or support these tools. Information for a flipped classroom session must be prepared, structured, and visually represented. Design is everything. Concise content of 10–15 minutes is recorded in video format. Material can consist of live teaching video, YouTube material, and animated narrated slideshows. It must engage and be suitable for colleagues with varying experience levels. Sharp content takes time and practice to develop. Once complete it's re-usable. Involving senior executives or managers in producing sessions increases sponsorship and connection. Video and reference material is supplied via weblink so that colleagues can access material at home, on the move, or whenever it suits. For specialist topics a short piece of interactive eLearning can teach ideas, nuances, and decision making. The design of eLearning includes:

- ❖ context to connect the learner to the bigger picture;
- ❖ core learning information;
- ❖ a relatable challenge or problem for the learner to decide upon with three plausible and realistic responses, including the preferred answer;
- ❖ positive or negative consequences for each choice;
- ❖ all three responses may be plausible so there is often not an entirely wrong answer.

The classroom

At the working session the coach leads:

- ❖ quick, gamified assessments to check take-up of material;
- ❖ fishbowl sessions where volunteers work on an issue and others watch;
- ❖ practical skill development, using role play or simulation and immediate feedback;
- ❖ personalized guided learning as delegates attempt to apply learning;
- ❖ clarification discussions and debates to stimulate thinking;
- ❖ collaborative project work with coach support as requested;
- ❖ next-level learning material.

The working session may be a 15-minute discussion or a series of consecutive discussions through the course of a week or a workshop of one to three hours.

Create an extraordinary working experience

Transformation presents extraordinary challenge: the need to keep one job or procedure running in parallel with a new one, added complexity, new technology, learning of new skills – the list goes on. Why would anyone want this? It's too much work; business as usual is so much easier. Unless, that is, there is a way to transform working lives by providing an extraordinary working experience and an opportunity to produce amazing results. It was many years ago whilst watching my nephews playing video games (see below) that I realized the power of the peak performance trance; a moment when a person tunes out from the world and into their challenge with the side effect of outstanding results. I was struck by the potential for incredible results if it were possible to reproduce the circumstances at work.

The trance of peak performance

The game opens and players are thrust into a bewildering environment with no instruction. After a brief familiarization, trial, error, and a period of learning tips and techniques, they grasp the context and control the characters. Focus intensifies, the tools are intuitive, and they sense the adjustments required to succeed. Mistakes are many and feedback is instant. A distinctive sound signals the untimely demise of a character. There are no consequences or externally inflicted bad feelings, just internal frustration and a desire to try again. They start over, transfixed, with no sense of time or the presence of others, addicted to beating each other's scores. Each level adds new complexity, demanding more skill, yet the learning quickens. A challenge is conquered, a brief celebration, and the cycle repeats. Interrupting the players, even to eat, will not break the spell. At last play is over and the top scorer basks in the glory of peer recognition, their performance displayed atop a league table. Incessant performance autopsy and the exhilaration of mastery generate hunger for the next more challenging alternative.

It turns out that this performance trance has a name; it's the state of 'Flow', a term coined by Mihaly Csikszentmihalyi in his work on creating happiness.[39] Several conditions and their consequences create the *Flow* state:

Conditions

1. A stretching challenge and matching skills.
2. Clear goals and feedback.
3. A sense of personal control over the activity.
4. Intense, distraction-free focus in the present moment.
5. A sense of potential to succeed.

Consequences

1. Merging of action and awareness (body and mind).
2. A loss of self-consciousness.
3. A distorted experience of time.
4. Experience of the activity as intrinsically rewarding.
5. Sacrifice of personal needs to engrossment in the experience.

We all have the potential to experience more flow, because of the natural pharmacy in our brain. Three important neurotransmitters

---

[39] Mihaly Csikszentmihalyi, *Flow: The Psychology of Optimal Experience*, Rider, 2002.

provide the DNA of peak performance.[40] *Dopamine* is the fun chemical; it updates the memory and affects the ability to focus. It's also linked to motor skills and produces a reward that makes us want more. *Noradrenaline* is the hormone that gives us the rush when we do something scary. It regulates attention and alertness for survival. Higher levels lead to greater accuracy. Noradrenaline peaks when we feel slightly over challenged or push ourselves to perform a difficult task better, faster, or with fewer resources. *Acetylcholine* is the chemical which sharpens focus. It must be activated by making a conscious effort to pay attention, during exercise or when we are exposed to something new or important. Noradrenaline gets our attention, dopamine engages us, and acetylcholine sharpens our focus.

Finding flow

Work may not appear to be as constraint free and conducive to flow as games or sports, but studies show that many people report their flow experiences occurring at work where goals are clear, and challenge is available in abundance. Transformation offers the ultimate example of increasingly complex challenge. Just as we master one element, the challenge grows and pushes us to the edge of our experience. Finding flow starts with attitude: the ability to view challenges with potential for enjoyment rather than opportunities to fail and be judged. Some personalities are too self-conscious, critical, or unable to focus. Others experience flow easily and can focus attention and see every opportunity for mastery. If we channel the right thoughts, we increase the chance of finding flow experiences. A leader can cultivate the attitude to flow by fostering the right environment: removing distractions,

---

[40] Friederike Fabritius and Hans W. Hagemann, *The Leading Brain: Neuroscience Hacks to Work Smarter, Better, Happier*, TarcherPerigee, 2018, pp. 3–26.

encouraging reduced self-consciousness, reacting to mistakes with coaching, and working with clear goals. Open access to the flow experience by matching a person to the task, and gradually increasing complexity to promote growth. Pay attention to the working environment, communication, organizational goals, and how teams are put together and supported. Make it possible for each person to bring their best self to work and be free to use their strengths, experiment, express themselves, and apply their creativity. The following is an example of one such approach to increasing access to flow.

Pleasure, passion, and pride

In a European business, my team and I launched the 'Make a Difference' campaign, which challenged leaders to create an environment where teams could achieve extraordinary experience through pleasure of using their strengths autonomously, passion from a connection to the mission and opportunity to achieve mastery, and pride from recognition of great work. Leaders were trained as active leaders to upgrade their ability to relate to the team, communicate, recognize, and deploy strengths. A 'pick and mix' selection of tools were offered for working with their team on one or more of six themes, depending upon the needs suggested by engagement survey results: Communication and Involvement; Feedback and Training; Relationship with Manager; Opportunity to Progress; Recognition; and Teamwork. Leaders accepted the challenge and worked inclusively with their team to address gaps. Initiatives provided an environment where flow was possible. In outperforming groups, employees described greater incidences of enjoyable challenges which tested their skills and engagement scores increased by between 15% and 25%.

Engaging a team for transformation

The flow concept and engagement framework have proved repeatedly successful in enhancing engagement and are adapted into a memorable system to drive engagement for transformation: the CIRCLE of TRUST, set out below.

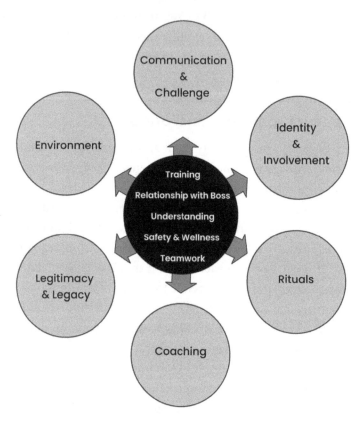

Figure 16: CIRCLE of TRUST system

Communication and challenge

Communication

Minimize anxieties through clear communication at the outset, answering questions and providing opportunities for dialogue. Set up communication disciplines and routines. Invest resources for high-quality communication. Use frequent pulse check surveys to assess the climate and gauge concerns which need a response. Start with who we are, why we exist, what we need to do, and ways in which the team contribute to the success of the programme and the organization. People can change in an instant but only when presented with an idea that jars, topples their existing belief, and creates a new one. Dissatisfaction grows, building energy and urgency for action. Anticipate and address personal fears in all phases of communication to prevent performance dips and damaging behaviour.

Challenge

People perform best when challenged; they relish their success when they win through a hard-fought battle of demands in a busy, uncertain environment. Challenge means pushing the boundaries of experience and learning through stretching standards. Understand strengths and skills, deploy them well, and work them harder. If the task is too easy, apathy, boredom, and distraction result. Test and flex goals, knowing when to step in with course corrections and step out to allow experimentation. Immediacy of feedback and the freedom to use judgement and make mistakes is a balance to be sought in pursuit of flow.

Identity and involvement

Identity

Our job and career are part of our identity, the sense of purpose and significance that keep us moving forward. When something messes with this, we become anxious and protective. The fears generated by change create an influx of hormones. Cortisol flows, driving up blood pressure, and adrenaline dampens the immune system. When fears prevail, people move into persistent fight or flight mode with symptoms of stress. The question of identity is addressed by carefully disrupting beliefs and creating new and better ones. Traditional change management focuses on external factors of environment, results, behaviours, and resources, all of which are important. It is, however, the internal transformation of people – their values, beliefs, and identity – that creates true change. See Dilts model of neurological levels in Chapter 4.

Becoming world class

When transforming one team, momentum and mindset for change were built during one year by sharing a vision of the future organization, assigning the target of 'Becoming World Class', and highlighting the chasm between the current and future state. Frequent messaging and a development programme prepared the community, whilst communication and training enhanced the strengths and identity of the team. Small successes were reinforced, and with growing confidence, communications transitioned to a focus on 'fit for the future' and exploration of unproductive methods. Ambition for new skills and method increased through exposure to external best practice. A transition conference connected the messaging of the previous year. Measurement of delegate engagement, commitment before and after, indicated a significant mindset shift. The few days of 'connecting dots' and allowing messages to coalesce in their minds changed the future. Inclusiveness, sequence, and intensity of communications created ownership. The team elected to migrate from a federally dissipated group towards a unified, world-class team. Their mission was to provide exceptional strategic and operational support to the achievement of business results. An identity they could proudly adopt.

Involvement

Sharing information and including people in decision making is a sign of respect, which increases feelings of significance and control. It offers choices, encourages connection with the vision and a more positive interpretation. With a stronger self-image, people view problems optimistically rather than negatively, focusing on what they can do rather than what they can't. Increase feelings of control through involvement at many levels: goal decisions, visioning, progress updates and more. When we hold a clear vision the brain sees it as an instruction, notices anything relevant and encourages action to make the vision real.

Rituals

Rituals are the result of habits, routines, and events that have evolved into enchanting, pleasurable moments of heightened focus; they are moments which quiet the mind, energize, and increase the sense of belonging. Through bonding and connection with others, focus, and flow, they improve wellbeing, enhance skills, and provide a source of resilience and positive team spirit.

The power of ritual

During school break in my teens, I worked gruelling split shifts, waiting tables at a conference centre. Each day at 10am the team of chefs, housekeepers and waiters assembled for a break; the calm before the storm, warmly anticipated after the bustle of the morning shift. The smell of coffee and food anchored the moment. Tales of the previous evening provided welcome distraction and mental refuelling, whilst an obligatory bout of humour and banter lifted spirits. Lost in our bubble for the moment, time passed quickly, until we were jolted reluctantly back to our priorities. The break always extended over time, yet managers never disrupted the ritual. They knew that the morale boost, team bonds, and renewed energy carried us through the long shift and ensured commitment and enthusiasm for work.

Rituals are best nurtured organically; they can lose their magic when imposed. The moment when a routine or habit turns into a ritual is subtle and difficult to spot. Explore breaks, regular routines, and events such as orientation, conferences, or meetings as potential start points. Inject fun, informality, mindfulness, discussion, or celebration. Use food and drink where possible to anchor the senses and build associations. It's possible to look at any aspect of the day and explore how to make it more mindful and meaningful.

Coaching

Leaders miss the opportunity to coach because they see it as time consuming or confrontational. If it is either of these, it's not coaching. Performance coaching is a priority for the team leader. Without dynamic coaching, sports or athletic teams could never win. Make coaching a normal everyday occurrence: brief observation, playback of facts, followed by the reflections of the employee and supporting discussion, are all it takes. Proximity to a coach and frequency of coaching are important for wellbeing. Analyse the team in progress, observe and reflect on what is and is not working, and get their attention whilst memories are vivid. The team and coach work together to dissect the performance, process the learning, and engage in improvement action and practice. See the 'A' GAME ON approach in Chapter 4.

Legitimacy and legacy

Change ejects everyone from their comfort zone. It's not unusual to experience the feeling that the work has no purpose or that we, or our skills, don't fit with a situation or a team. This inner conflict is the result of competing claims on attention and many incompatible goals. Restore team focus, feelings of authenticity, and sense of impact. It starts with personal connection to the vision and plan, together with clear goals, as we saw in Chapter 3. It requires involvement, and a culture where the team have meaningful debate about work and reinforce their sense of progress and contribution; see Chapter 6. Use tools to identify skills, personality, styles, and strengths, as we saw in Chapter 2. Grow confidence in capability. Peer recognition activities reinforce significance by encouraging team members to discuss and describe others' contributions. See the Dynamic team 360 process described in Chapter 5.

Environment

A comfortable non-threatening environment provides a physical and psychological space for people to fulfil their potential. It's made up of physical rooms, layouts, resources for work and leisure, and intangible features: communication styles, team dynamics, meetings, personnel policies, accountability mechanisms, and management relationships. The environment design sets up the circumstances for peak performance, engagement, and flow. Pay attention to the cleanliness, attractiveness, and safety of facilities. Consider how communication works, how managers make themselves visible and accessible, and the availability of performance information. Check out what gets celebrated, key events, how opportunities for development and progression are accessed, and how recognition happens. When resources are scarce and so long as safety needs are taken care of, prioritize intangible factors affecting relationships before workplace aesthetics.

Training

Learning is the most natural rewarding instinct we have; anyone who has mastered a new skill will recognize the dopamine high they experience. We are programmed to solve problems and retain knowledge for future benefit through the neural pathways that we build and strengthen. Building a learning culture and finding opportunities for people to learn creatively at work increase connection to the work, maintain interest, and reignite challenge. Training and learning are accessible due to new technology, if we design in the time to learn and help with processing of information. Opportunities for practice, reflection, experimentation, and play are all nectar to the brain's learning activation centre.

Relationship with boss, recognition, and the progress principle

Connection with the boss affects our daily happiness, livelihood, performance, and personal life. When we value our boss and they value us, and notice what we do, we feel competent and supported. An imbalance in mutuality of respect and trust has performance consequences. The manager's ability to pay attention and acknowledge contribution boosts performance if it is specific, descriptive, and non-judgemental. Practise the simple and effective art of observing and describing. Consider the difference between 'That was good' versus 'I watched how you handled that difficult situation, and I noticed the consultative technique you used to bring the other party around'. Even more significant than recognition is the effect of seeing progress in our work. A study by Teresa Amabile and Steven Kramer of Harvard University revealed how events that signify progress in work like small wins, breakthroughs, and goal completion have the most significant impact on inner work life, and therefore the performance and creativity of individuals.[41] Noticing the person, facilitating and marking progress, course correcting, dynamic feedback, and recognition are simple, involve little time, and are the most powerful tools a manager can use.

---

[41] Teresa Amabile and Steven Kramer, *The Progress Principle: Using Small Wins to Ignite Joy, Engagement, and Creativity at Work*, Harvard Business Review Press, 2011.

Understanding

Empathy is the ability to understand the consequences of our actions for others, or to see the world through their eyes. Some people appear to be missing an empathy 'chip'; workload pressures can dumb down the empathy radar. If empathy doesn't come easily, use checklists, stakeholder lists, and force routines which enquire about others' needs. Ask the team how they are, what challenges they face, and what help they require.

Compassion, from the Latin *compati* which means suffering together, is about understanding the challenges faced by a person with the intention to alleviate their suffering. It can be considered too soft for some leaders when difficult decisions demand a hard, dispassionate approach. On the contrary, acts of compassion cost nothing, increase engagement in those who observe it, and provide physical and psychological health benefits for givers and receivers. Compassion is a survival instinct; humans and animals demonstrate compassionate behaviour even before it's taught. Charles Darwin in his work on 'The descent of man and selection in relation to sex' commented that communities with the greatest number of sympathetic members would flourish best and rear more offspring.[42] Studies show that the act of giving compassion appears to be as pleasurable, if not more so, than the act of receiving. Showing compassion helps us enjoy better mental and physical health and speeds up recovery from disease.

Safety and wellness

Safety

A safe, comfortable work environment and an active concern for wellness communicate care and affect the way people feel about their job and employer. Employees face high work demands,

---

[42] Charles R. Darwin, *The Descent of Man, and Selection in Relation to Sex*, Digireads.com, 2009, p. 110.

limited resources, relationship problems, and other environmental factors which contribute to mental and physical illness. Identifying and removing physical and often camouflaged psychological risks is ground zero. A motivating learning experience for one person may cause anxiety in another. How can we determine when work demands are excessive or merely challenging, or whether relationships are good or toxic? How do we know when remote and home working provide life balance or isolation, or when a performance measurement technology increases focus or anxiety? The answer lies in a transparent culture, where leaders believe in and prioritize safety and wellness; safe habits, routines, and training are ingrained and reinvigorated regularly; lapses aren't tolerated for a minute; people speak out and challenge without fear; and a respectful and safety-focused style is rewarded.

Wellness

Wellness is 'the feeling of optimal balance between emotional, psychological, physical and spiritual health'.[43] Wellness needs for one person may be about relationships, for another, nutrition or physical health – a hint that trying to find a solution is a minefield. Some organizations use a 'sheep dip' solution, although evidence suggests this is not solving the problem. In fact, where companies introduce lunch-time yoga, massage, and mindfulness sessions, expecting that everyone will benefit, they can sometimes have the opposite effect. This is not to say that such interventions aren't positive, well-intentioned, or good for some people, but dealing with wellness starts with culture. Does the organization value people who seem to work all hours or place pressure on people to be seen to be working 24/7? Do people suffer with Sunday-night anxiety or fill with dread on sight of an email in the inbox? Do people have choice in the way they work? What support is available for employees juggling work and home responsibilities?

---

[43] Alice Fraser, 'All being well: A brief history of wellness', Audible podcast, 2020.

Mental and physical wellbeing keep a team running on all cylinders, feeling healthy, relaxed, and in control of emotions, whilst fatigue, excess stress, mental or physical pain diminish motivation and confidence. See Transformation and mental health below.

1. Assess stressors in organizational culture and the inner work life of employees – the UK HSE Management Standards Indicator Tool can help.
2. Review and implement a wellness strategy.
3. Review/develop policies – e.g., flexible working, vacation, performance management.
4. Develop leaders in supportive and respectful leadership.
5. Educate people in wellness and embed reflection, relaxation, and planning time.
6. Invest in stress management and increase awareness of mindfulness and meditation.
7. Train leaders and supervisors in coaching and feedback skills.
8. Encourage physical exercise and healthy nutrition.
9. Train in time and task management.
10. Increase awareness and access to therapies – for a summary of some key therapies, visit transform2outperform.com

Teamwork

A sense of team connection, support, and loyalty contribute to happiness at work; our success is possible through collaboration and constructive relationships. We all recall the effects of being supported by a team in completing work or the impact of being obstructed at every turn. Collaboration and team working during transformation are critical because of complexity, uncertainty, heightened emotions, and new performance dynamics. Understand that teams find their performance sweet spot over time. Invest in team development, starting with careful selection to ensure a balance of skills, personalities, and diversity, as we saw earlier. Facilitate conflict resolution, encourage and reward collaborative behaviours within and across teams, and provide tools, teamwork training, and the freedom to decide about work.

In summary, to find flow and create the extraordinary employee experience develop the CIRCLE of TRUST. One size does not fit all. Engagement effort must be continuous, personalized, and second nature. Be a boss the team can learn from; develop empathy with each team member and recognize their most important needs. Be mindful that some are motivated by skills and career, desperate to be the best; others want to increase their wealth, life balance, and vacation time; others love the extraordinary work experience and connecting with the team. Some people just want to exceed their own, and your, expectations.

Transformation and mental health

Whether participant or passive recipient to transformation, the pressure to do more in less time and maintain current performance whilst running new methods can detrimentally impact mental, physical, and emotional health. Training is often underestimated or fails to prepare those affected. Anxieties include the fear of job loss, inability to perform in the new environment, loss of expertise and power base, dislike of new methods, and changes to team dynamics. Anxieties can turn into unhealthy, unproductive behaviours. The following case study demonstrates the dangers of missing poor mental health.

Hidden danger

Sally worked for an international business in a senior executive role. The first year was tough but she built a team, turned around underperforming operations, and made a difference. A self-assured and sociable person, she was able to build good relationships. Three years in, she was popular with her peer group and felt safe, powerful, and important.

She enjoyed great work–life balance, a busy social life, and a happy marriage. Flying high and recognized as such with rewards and responsibilities, ebullience, occasional arrogance, and sensitivity to feedback hinted at the importance she placed on her status. The previous year had been challenging when Sally sat down for a routine meeting with her boss, expecting to debate topical issues. Thirty minutes later she marched out of the building, never to return. Her boss had decided to reorganize, with the consequence that her prized role would be demoted under the leadership of a colleague. She felt shocked as she had not seen any warning signs. The feelings of betrayal, injustice, and indignity were immense. She left, and a bitter battle ensued. Five months later, Sally signed a settlement with her former employer. Finally, closure, she could move on. It was a warm spring Monday, hinting at a beautiful summer to come. Sally savoured her morning coffee with the family and said goodbye. She had much to do before starting her new role in a few short weeks. She closed the door, tidied around, and strode into the garage, whereupon she secured a rope to a beam and promptly took her own life, leaving a tsunami of devastation.

Could a reorganization alone be enough to bring about the end of a full and valued life? What could have caused a capable, self-assured person to take that most fateful step? The loss of status and a job, or were other things at play here? No one will ever know Sally's state of mind during those final days and hours. We do know however, that her spouse, friends, colleagues, or boss will forever wonder whether they could have prevented this dreadful outcome. Sadly, this is based on a true story. It's an indication of how career and the perceptions of others become an enormous part of a person's life and sense of self. Thankfully, most people who suffer poor mental health do not take their own lives. Many do suffer reduced quality of life and health with a compounding effect on family and friends. If nothing else, this story is a brutal reminder of the need to lead and manage the lives of others with care, compassion, dignity, and respect. Work-related causes of poor mental health include burnout, exhaustion, poor working conditions, bullying, inequality, a competitive environment, hire and fire culture, toxic relationships, chronic pain, long-term sickness, injustice, job loss, discrimination, harassment, and more. Fortunately, developments in neuroscience and positive psychology offer tools for retraining the brain and strategies for life improvement. Wellbeing of employees will become a top leadership priority during the next decade.

Software of the mind

Ground-breaking studies show how some psychological characteristics like depression, disposition for suicide, anxiety, addiction, and fear conditioning are inheritable.[44] Our genes can be given biological markers by our parents' experience and passed down a generation. Experiments on mice and other animals have shown how parents can be conditioned to fear certain things, which is passed down to their offspring without them having been exposed to the stimulus or condition. These changes can last for up to two generations. This field of science is called epigenetics. The Greek prefix 'epi' means 'over, outside of', therefore literally 'on top of genes'. It explores how genes are activated. Some genes have an inherited and predetermined development and activation; they express themselves as nature has provided. Certain genes, however, express themselves in response to experience and environmental factors; they are effectively dialled up or down depending upon the quality of our lives. Our entire cellular biology can, it seems,

---

[44] Martha Henriques, 'Can the legacy of trauma be passed down the generations?', *BBC*, 26 March 2019. Available from www.bbc.com/future/article/20190326-what-is-epigenetics [accessed 19 May 2022].

change with the *flick of a thought* triggered by our experience and interpretation. The work environment can, therefore, have a very real effect on quality of life. As leaders we can't be responsible for a genetic trait that disposes someone to mental health problems, and we can't remove the reality of work demands or second-guess everyone's mental capacity. We can minimize factors which activate those genes by providing choice, support, altering interpretation or dampening negative experiences through a wellness strategy.

Stress is good for you

It's well known that stress contributes to serious ill health, so the idea that 'stress is good for us' jars immediately. Let's explore this counterintuitive idea. First, the stress response is a natural bio-logical process that motivates us to act; it can help our perfor-mance and ensure we stay safe. We know that stress hormones are released in the positive, peak-performing state of flow when faced with a challenge that stretches our capabilities. Science now tells us that something as simple as changing your mind about stress and interpreting it as positive instead of bad can change your body's response to it. One study tracked 30,000 adults over eight years and concluded that, where people experienced significant stress in the last year, there was a 43% increased risk of dying; however, this was only true for the people who *also believed that stress is harmful for your health*.[45] People who experienced a lot of stress but did not view stress as harmful were no more likely to die. They had the lowest risk of dying of anyone in the study, including people who had relatively little stress.[46] Researchers estimated that through-

---

[45] Kelly McGonigal, 'How to make stress your friend', TED Global 2013, June 2013. Available from www.ted.com/talks/kelly_mcgonigal_how_to_make_stress_your_friend [accessed 19 May 2022].
[46] Abiola Keller et al., 'Does the perception that stress affects health matter? The association with health and mortality', *Health Psychology*, 2012;31(5): 677–684.

out the eight years they were tracking, 182,000 people died prematurely, not from stress, *but from the belief that stress is bad for you.*[47] Another study looked at the combination of stress and time spent caring for others. The study concluded that for every major stressful life experience, like a family crisis or financial problems, the risk of dying increased by 30%, but people who spent time caring for others showed no stress-related increase in dying,[48] – an overwhelming incentive for leaders to take responsibility for the wellness of their teams.

Mind–body connection

A leader comments to her team 'I am going to spend time with each of you; I want to understand current performance in the team'. Helen, a long-serving team member, assumes her performance is under question. In her head she re-runs instances where she felt a failure and makes assumptions about how the manager is aware of this. Before she knows it, she is lost in her thoughts, feeling under attack, and disconnected from the rest of the meeting. Helen searches her memory for defensive evidence to share with the manager. She experiences emotions which cause an adrenaline rush and a drop of dopamine, pushing up blood pressure and forcing blood flow to her limbs and amygdala. As adrenaline subsides, cortisol, another steroidal hormone, flows pushing glucose into the bloodstream for energy, suppressing the immune system, regulating metabolism, influencing neural pathway development and memory creation. She begins to mind read and hypothesize

[47] Jeremy P. Jamieson et al., 'Mind over matter: Reappraising arousal improves cardiovascular and cognitive responses to stress', *Journal of Experimental Psychology*, 2012;141(3): 417–422.

[48] Michael J. Poulin, Stephanie L. Brown, Amanda J. Dillard, and Dylan M. Smith, 'Giving to others and the association between stress and mortality', *American Journal of Public Health*, 2013;103(9): 1649–1655.

the manager's motive. Her senses become acute, allowing her to dream up negative consequences. She experiences a burst of oxytocin, a stress hormone that will encourage her to reach out and seek comfort through connection.

Jack, the newest member of the team, sees the manager's comment as positive. He is fascinated by the session and excited about the follow-up meeting. He listens carefully and feels he knows what's driving the manager. A burst of adrenaline and cortisol and a drop of dopamine motivate him to prepare for the meeting with his achievements. He too benefits from endorphins, the body's natural opiates (pain de-sensitizers), which leave him with a feeling of wellbeing. Oxytocin fine tunes his social instincts and primes him to strengthen relationships; he feels connected to the manager. A serotonin blast makes him feel important.

Personality traits predispose a more optimistic or pessimistic outlook, and specific skills or experiences affect how the individuals in the above case study rationalize the situation. The consequences are distinct. Neither Jack nor Helen have the complete picture of the situation. Let's assume the manager has concerns about performance. Who will be better prepared, Jack or Helen? Jack has maintained focus; his approach will be positive and constructive. He has absorbed more of the manager's presentation and will be prepared if problems are raised. Helen may appear defensive by homing in on things she feels bad about, thereby risking the appearance of incompetence. The behaviour becomes self-fulfilling.

The simple thought process causes a negative or positive psychological and physical impact on the individual. The mind and body are connected. Jack's response full of endorphins reduces cardiovascular stress, improves the immune system, and reduces likelihood of stress-related health symptoms. The constantly elevated stress hormones designed for emergency use put Helen at risk of headache and insomnia. The effects of remaining on high alert create an overload of adrenaline and cortisol and begin to affect her sleep cycle and immune system. She becomes a candidate for cardiovascular disease, depression, gastrointestinal problems, and other illnesses caused by inflammation in the body, raised blood pressure, and low endorphins. This is the biology of belief.[49] Internal and environmental factors produce biological markers or proteins which switch on certain genes and can lead to diseases like cancer or diabetes.

Is there any hope for Helen with her pessimistic, paranoid personality? It's true that personality characteristics like pessimism and hostility are correlated with levels of disease and premature death; thankfully, however, there are strategies which can help.

Changing habits

Increasing awareness of the tendency to overreact can tone down reactions. Strategies for coping include teaching Helen to ask clarifying questions, practising positive re-framing. A pessimistic personality has a lifetime of practice and may need help recognizing triggers, emotional and behavioural routines, and subtle intrinsic rewards for limiting behaviour which ensure it is repeated. She will need to practise a different routine and reward many times before a new habit is formed.

Adopting a stress buddy

Helen's colleagues and boss can help her to see where she adopts a negative approach and to achieve a balanced perspective. Stress buddies help each other build confidence and resilience. Hugging a colleague, with their consent, produces oxytocin, increasing the sense of connection and support.

---

[49] Bruce Lipton, *The Biology of Belief: Unleashing the Power of Consciousness, Matter & Miracles*, Hay House UK, 2015.

Changing belief

Training Helen to see that the stress response can be good for her, helping restructure her response and associate her physical reactions with excitement instead of anxiety will decrease negative effects. She *must truly believe* this for it to work; it will take time and reinforcement.

Small leadership tweaks

Helen's boss can upgrade communication, break big goals into smaller ones, acknowledge progress, give regular feedback, and create new challenge to eliminate anxiety and keep dopamine flowing. By pointing out the significance of roles, reflecting on achievements, and practising gratitude, her boss will boost confidence, increasing serotonin and a sense of purpose. Outdoor breaks and physical exercise will also provide a serotonin shot. Using team events to encourage social interactions filled with a sense of community, humour, and relaxation creates bonds and stimulates oxytocin. Encouraging work/home balance, self-compassion, and the practice of relaxation and mindfulness techniques are hallmarks of respectful leadership.

The biology of belief can help us derive the positive benefits from stress so long as surroundings are conducive.

Practising focus

Focus is possible through intense practice, which builds confidence in the ability to perform in any situation and offers access to flow. It involves making a conscious decision to concentrate and stay on point, narrowing focus onto manageable tasks rather than multitasking, keeping head and body in the same place by doing and thinking about the same thing, avoiding uncontrollable distractions, and keeping attention outward rather than inward.

High-performing symbiotic teams

So far, we have discovered that people power is released when capable people occupy the right roles, and we create the conditions for success, including a focus on supporting mental health. There are, however, additional considerations. To turbo boost people power, the right team must be combined with the right leader and culture; see Chapter 6. It's accepted wisdom that high-performance teams embody a compelling shared purpose, have clearly defined roles, ambitious goals, open communication, a continuous improvement process, and a strong leader who brings all this into being. These factors are already the subject of many leadership books; however, I have always felt that we are missing something about leaders and their teams who achieve unrivalled success. After studying the results and style of such leaders and their teams, I discovered the SYMBIOTIC interplay of the team, their leader and certain leadership actions which boost people power and results.

Symbiosis

Symbiosis is a biological term used to describe the cooperative partnership which develops between organisms, helping creatures to innovate and expand into new places. These relationships, often between competing or conflicting organisms, form to solve problems and go on to create emergent properties or consequences through the exchange of DNA or other material. In the tropical regions of Africa, the crocodile lies with its mouth open and the Egyptian plover flies inside to feed on decaying meat stuck in the crocodile's teeth. The crocodile doesn't eat the plover; it enjoys the benefit of free dental treatment. Likewise, humans host trillions of bacteria like lactobacillus in the gut, which help to digest a wide variety of food in exchange for a place to live, with emergent properties that prevent obesity and other serious diseases. This natural process describes the conditions that must occur in a high-performing team: a mutually beneficial dependence on each other which releases value over and above that of the individuals themselves.

A symbiotic team in action

As we explore the characteristics of a SYMBIOTIC team, try to apply them to your favourite outperforming team. There's no better example than the widely reported failed moon mission of Apollo 13. The astronauts faced unimaginable danger, yet their experience, knowledge, intensive training, and time spent together as a team ensured they were able to navigate in space without their usual resources. The calm, decisive, and motivational role played by Jim Lovell, the team's commander, was vital. Back in Houston, teams of experts showed incredible commitment, clear thinking, and capacity to perform. The absence of ego and courage of conviction in speaking out about risks, demonstrated by individuals under pressure, was critical. Team members alternated between specialist accountabilities and working together to solve complex, unanticipated problems in record time: how to separate a lunar module from a command module before re-entry, how to produce an air filtration system out of components available on the ship, and how to conserve power for re-entry into the earth's atmosphere. Not to forget the heroic and calm leadership of Flight Director Gene Krantz, whose unfailing confidence, and insistence that failure was not an option, challenged the team to deliver; famously proclaiming that 'this would be our (NASA's) finest hour'. Indeed, the safe return of three astronauts in the context of the most extraordinary challenge was an extraordinary achievement by an extraordinary team. So let's explore the characteristics of a SYMBIOTIC team and its leader.

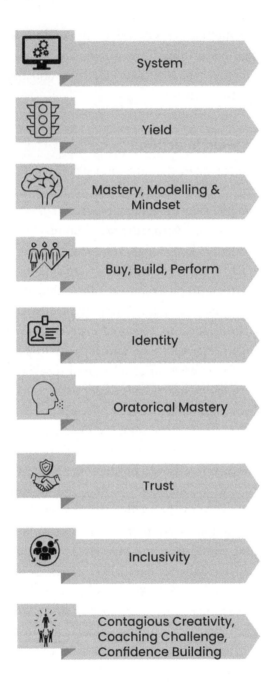

Figure 17: SYMBIOTIC team

System

It's not often that a skilled team becomes high performing by virtue of just being together; there must be a method to the performance. The task is to combine team skills and strengths in a simple system that allows them to achieve the intangible, intuitive synergy which competitors struggle to emulate. Simplify the task, break it into parts, and assign clear accountability. With practice and a system, each team member fulfils their role at supersonic pace and intuitive coordination. A Formula One race team define a system, clarify roles, and work relentlessly to improve routines, timings, ability to read the performance of the car and road conditions, and the driver. This means they can identify and solve problems in real time or change a tyre or part within seconds or fractions of a second. Making the complex simple is why leaders are leaders; it's not easy to do. The simplicity of approach demonstrated by the greatest performers is striking, yet they are people who waded through a sea of complexity to find the solution. When Ray Kroc (profiled in Chapter 6) founded McDonald's Inc., he had processed years of experience to filter the simple concepts which now make up the operating model of the fast-food industry. Leaders are code breakers; they must find their way to the simple answer and maintain focus and conviction despite the critics.

Yield

Teamwork involves a willingness to yield, to let go or forgo something for the benefit of the other or the team in return for the same courtesy. This yielding to the system and coaching of the leader allows other team members to fulfil their part of the task. It helps to hone intuitive reactions between the team members.

Mastery, modelling, and mindset

Mastery

A symbiotic team has a growth mindset, which helps them try harder and achieve more. This involves a belief by the coach and the team in their ability to achieve great things, however low their starting point. The target never stands still; competitors change and environmental conditions present new situations to master. The team constantly level up, moving through stages of apprenticeship, active creativity, experimenting, observing others, discussing failure, and overcoming challenges. The coach and team compare performances, identify strengths or past achievements, and tap in to the accompanying feelings and conditions of performance so that they can be repeated and improved upon. The team see overall improvement when the less experienced witness and engage with the skill and performance of senior members; it boosts their confidence and desire to act.

Modelling

Identifying other role models and imagining their reactions, attitudes, and methods is a performance mastery resource. The technique offers access to creativity a person may not otherwise display. Research shows that the brain distinguishes little between our own actions and those of others we witness or imagine. In the company of others, our brain continuously mirrors the behaviour displayed around us. These mirror neurons provide the basis for empathy and all human communication. As Giacomo Rizzolatti,[50] the Italian scientist said, 'Mirror neurons allow us to grasp the minds of others not through conceptual reasoning but through direct stimulation. By feeling, not by thinking'. Acting out the role or emulating the thoughts of another creates emotional experience and wires the neurons of the brain differently for performance.

---

[50] Giacomo Rizzolatti and Corrado Sinigaglia, *Mirrors in the Brain: How Our Minds Share Actions and Emotions*, Oxford University Press, 2008.

Help the team to identify role models and select aspects of their style, thought process, or approach to adopt.

Mindset

Performance is a win, a goal scored, a presentation delivered, a transformation. When we recall great performances, we think of actors like Jack Nicholson in *The Shining*, or perhaps a moving speech comes to mind: President Kennedy's 'we choose to go to the Moon…' Or Martin Luther King's 'I have a dream'. These portrayals and events are memorable because, by combining crafted words, careful pacing, and tonality, they embody authenticity and character. It's easy to miss the fact that these seemingly effortless performances have been refined and rehearsed endlessly, sometimes through a lifetime of experience. Similarly, we remember teams who stormed a championship or two. Their performances mesmerize with skill, speed and flow of play, and an intuitive responsiveness between players. Whilst the words used, the skills, and method of delivery are important, the critical factor in these performances is the physiological state adopted by the performers; the emotions and mental capacity required to achieve focus and apply themselves consistently, regardless of the challenge. Great performers have a mentality or mindset, an orientation or hunger for winning, for being the best and getting to the top. It's an 'on stage everyday mentality' supported by habits and rituals.

Supporting the performance mindset

Whilst accepted wisdom in the sporting world, a performance mindset may not come naturally in business. The culture that breeds this mindset takes time and incurs 'downtime'. Treat the project like a major sporting event that must be won; take time to define the terms of winning, the purpose, and the width of the goalposts. Find the talent and invest in their development as part of a team. Top talent are irrelevant without their supporting team. Superheroes become recognized as such through the contributions of their team and their role forged within a team. Facilitate the rituals and routines of pre- and post-performance and create the environment for a performance mindset to take root.

- ❖ Work with the team to develop purpose and vision. Focus on offering something unique or of exceptional value.
- ❖ Complete an intensive period of collaborative project definition. This 'downtime' will speed up successful performance.
- ❖ Run pre- and post-performance sessions, weekly or daily meetings which maintain team focus and ensure mental preparation for performance and advance handling of risks.
- ❖ Build in relaxation periods and opportunities for team connection. Build confidence and show faith in the team and individuals.
- ❖ Maintain radio contact with every team member; stay tuned to their motivation, wellbeing, and focus level. Always keep the 'airwaves' open.
- ❖ Agree on habits of performance and the bad ones that must be removed. Focus on creating a strong sense of ownership and a positive team spirit.
- ❖ Use existing knowledge or wisdom wherever necessary; don't create complexity where none is needed.

Activating a performance mindset

Before performance

- ❖ Reconnect with the purpose to align the team and remove personal agendas. Why are we doing this? What is our purpose? Who will be impacted?
- ❖ Maintain clear vision of the goal, the performance, how it should play out, who will do what, the scenarios to be confronted, and what you as a performer or leader will need to do. Just like watching a movie ahead of time,

witness the physical expressions of the characters; imagine the feelings and emotions at play. Forming and recalling the picture frequently imprints the future state in the mind and motivates action.

- ❖ Research every aspect of the performance to update capability. Use knowledge of earlier experience and competitor performers. Know what you must do to outperform.
- ❖ Practise constantly. Peak performance is preceded by intense capability development evolved through gradually increasing the level of challenge.
- ❖ Maintain mental and physical preparation. Run routines to improve focus, sense of control, and the ability to achieve an energized yet relaxed state. Maintain a healthy lifestyle, managing nutrition, exercise, and stress.
- ❖ Warm up. Refresh confidence by revisiting examples of earlier success, their accompanying conditions, and mental states. Watch footage of Jack Nicholson preparing to take on his iconic moment in *The Shining* as he pumps himself up in readiness for the shot.

During performance

- ❖ Focus on process, not the outcome. Good preparation allows the performer to achieve flow through intense concentration on technique and process. Keep the mind and body focused on the same thing, staying present in the moment, zoning out distractions, preventing background conversations in the mind, and focusing on the next stage of performance.
- ❖ Access the trance of peak performance – an altered state of consciousness in which the attention is narrowed at the sweet spot where competence and challenge meet. Distractions and noises fade into the distance; time appears to slow as effort and skill are targeted at the process. The

unconscious mind monitors the environment for threats and draws from the back catalogue of practice and experience to provide an intuitive response: the sudden spark of creativity in the moment, the amazingly returned lob by a tennis player, the intuitive decision making of a computer gamer, the stunning improvisation of an actor or musician or the critical decision of a business leader. Not only is creativity increased during the trance of peak performance, the state of flow, but it also continues for up to three days afterwards, according to a study led by Harvard professor Teresa Amabile.

After performance

- ❖ Cool down. Apply the same mental and physical discipline at the end of a performance to maintain a healthy attitude and avoid negative thinking. There may be issues to address, particularly if things have gone badly. Mental health deteriorates when we can't recover from setbacks or re-frame the outcome in a constructive light. Post-performance review and leadership support are crucial.
- ❖ Process the performance through reflection, discussion, reconstruction, and experimentation. The cognitive and sensory engagement embeds the experience, increases associations, and improves recall at critical moments. Treat every day as a practice for a moment of greatness.

Buy, build, perform

Shape and re-shape the team until the chemistry of the talent is right. Know when and how to shuffle the deck to create a new performance curve. A team requires constant honing of individual skills and refinement of style and system to fit the circumstances. Dissect the challenge faced, match team member strengths to the task, and recognize gaps in experience. Know when to inject experience and maturity or to bring new energy, creativity, and hunger by sourcing new people. Each time a new member joins the team, synergy is disrupted, and the team must rebuild. Achieving optimum performance is a perpetual cycle of buying the best, building the best, and performing the best. Individuals may fit the team at a certain point in time and fall out of fit at a different time; context matters. Messing with team synergy requires judgement and experience. To maintain respect and protect the performance of the team, the leader must know when turnover is required and must not change too slowly or quickly. Many a famous team or company have enjoyed stunning success, that is, until they were broken up too quickly. They must also treat the exit process with as much effort, integrity, and dignity as the buying process. As far as is possible, a team member must move on with high confidence, pride in their contribution, strong relationships with colleagues, and a sense of excitement for beginning a new performance curve.

Identity

People take pride, comfort, and safety in being part of a group. When individuals become members of a team, they are emboldened and empowered to take on a common challenger, enemy, or problem. Alliances form and bonds build, sometimes between characters who would otherwise not connect. The strong identification with a group builds aligned intentions and protective, supportive, and selfless behaviours. The success, power, and culture of a high-performing team attract new talent and fans.

Oratorical mastery

When a credible and authoritative leader publicly conveys an authentic belief in their team's ability to be successful, the team are inspired to believe in themselves. This must translate into individual coaching, learning advice, and the re-framing of experiences. Oratorical mastery is the magic that changes minds; it is achieved through stories, metaphors, words, language patterns, tonality, expressions, or movement to elicit a hypnotic, internal experience in the other person. On hearing the right words or stories the listener narrows focus, forms pictures, recalls associations, and becomes more suggestible. It is also the art of being able to say what others think but will not say.

Trust

Teams don't need to consist of people who love being together every waking hour, but they do require a common respect and sense of being able to depend on each other to get the job done. Trust is the foundation for performance in challenging situations, and allows the team to operate instinctively. Some relationships form overnight because of shared interests and chemistry, but they deepen and bond over time due to facing adversity together. The team's relationship with the leader is critical for creating the environment in which this can occur. Just as the leader orchestrates and directs the performance, matching individual strengths with roles and tasks, they also set up the challenge, enable practice, facilitate connections within the team, and embed relaxation and fun. If work is challenging and unpredictable, the team connect naturally in ways that can't be replicated. The difficulty, however, is that real-life situations create tension, pressure, and are a breeding ground for misunderstanding. The leader of a SYMBIOTIC team helps the team care for each other by working together on tasks, having fun, sharing personal vulnerability, understanding each other's strengths, and trusting each other. This investment prevents disconnection during real-life situations; it slashes decision-making time and is the difference between mediocrity and outperformance. A high-performing team faces relentless performance pressure. Simulation, relaxation, and fun are the release valve which dissipates tension and recentres the team. These leadership actions tighten relationship bonds and build a home where people want to live.

Inclusivity

When the team can influence priorities, have choices, and are consulted and involved in the development of a goal, their sense of commitment and responsibility is heightened. Every team member must understand their role and deliver their own specific contribution. The team must be able to challenge each other constructively to keep each other accountable. The balance between clarity of role and freedom to act independently is the result of accountability, discipline, teamwork, and practice.

Contagious creativity, coaching challenge, and confidence building

Contagious creativity

Albert Einstein is reported to have said 'creativity is contagious, pass it on'; it is instinctively true. We know that every time there's a new idea or technology, a new similar yet better one is created. The same can be said of talented teams. A team with a shared need or problem to solve, who train and spend time together, can achieve a level of performance greater than the sum of their contributions, a joint mastery. This organic creative flow is difficult to analyse and can only be overtaken by another team achieving the same state. Studies demonstrate the contagion of creativity and personal growth in team members who work with talented individuals.[51] The essence of contagious creativity is captured in a quote by Louise Fletcher, who played Nurse Ratchet in the movie *One Flew Over the Cuckoo's Nest*. She said about Jack Nicholson, 'He makes it look easy, but I can

---

[51] Teresa M. Amabile, 'Componential theory of creativity', April 2012. Available from www.hbs.edu/ris/Publication%20Files/12-096.pdf [accessed 19 May 2022].

assure you it isn't! He's just figured out a way to make it look like he's not giving you any effort whatsoever... He was there one hundred percent every day and made it so wonderful for everybody else too. They all got the bug of improvising and having fun with it and being inventive and creative'.[52] Symbiosis is the compound effect of learning from and building upon the confidence of each other, which ignites emergent talent and energy. Outside of the performance itself, members of a SYMBIOTIC team may appear unremarkable, yet, at their peak they are considered unbeatable. They have trained, bonded, and learned from each other to the extent that they can predict each other's responses and actions.

Coaching challenge

We discussed crucial conversations in the context of addressing performance shortfalls and fit. Coaching challenge is a type of crucial conversation. It uproots deep-seated issues and habits and drives a team to high performance. In this context, the leader creates discomfort by challenging the team. First and foremost, the leader supports and develops individual strengths, but they must also help the team to confront hard reality and be resilient to quick-fire, evaluative challenge. This is a positive process which confronts problems, holds the person accountable, and challenges thinking. It is from this place of discomfort that most teams step up their game. It can be used productively when the team have matured to a level of comfort with each other, respect their coach, and feel safe in the knowledge of their coach's support. SYMBIOTIC team leaders are exceptional at identifying the small details in performance. They use direct and challenging coaching with positive intention. They provide a supportive and

---

[52] Louise Fletcher cited in 'Jack Nicholson at 80: Life in pictures', *BBC Arts*. Available from. www.bbc.co.uk/programmes/articles/ 58DD9bbxm2rfPfFSLd1TZ&p/jack-nicholson-at-80-life-in-pictures [accessed 19 May 2022].

collegiate environment, attract respect for their experience and judgement, and focus on actions, facts, and results, not the person or physical attributes a person cannot change.

Confidence building

When a drug without active ingredients elicits a desired improvement, most notably in beating depression disorders, it is called a placebo effect. The combination of perceived *expertise and conviction* of the doctor prescribing the drug with the *expectation* that the drug contains the ingredients to solve the problem and that *something will change* causes the patient to experience a tangible improvement. Believable expectation of improvement combined with a person's capacity for self-improvement is the heart and soul of change. Many people don't understand their potential or talent until it's described to them by a boss or a teacher. With a few short words these mentors create a believable expectation, which primes the person to be alert to opportunities and decisions which fulfil the newfound belief. Ralph Waldo Emerson once said, 'Our chief want is someone who will inspire us to be what we know we could be'. If people know we expect great things from them, they go to great lengths to live up to our expectations. The brain tunes in to the vision and activates the natural seeking system, increasing motivation, focus, and curiosity. Psychotherapy techniques use perception and expectation as tools of influence and change. What we call 'confidence' is truly potent, the belief in our ability to think of a plan, act on it, and expect a successful outcome. A lack of confidence is equally powerful in its potential to destroy performance by reducing effort, willpower, and the willingness to focus on difficult goals. Confidence works in a spiral fashion; each success provides a boost, unlocking greater performance, whilst one or two failures can send it helter skeltering down. When a person feels good about their abilities, contribution, physical and mental health, and their leader's ability to coach, they have higher confidence in their own success, perceive competitive factors to be in their favour and tasks to be challenging rather than threatening, expect a better result, and are less negative when things get in the way.

Confident leadership style

Building confidence in the team starts with confident leadership. A confident leader style involves:

❖ **Poise** – upright stature and calm, controlled, thoughtful movements. Amy Cuddy in her book *Presence*[53] popularized the term 'fake it till you make it' after she and her colleagues demonstrated a link between power posture and the growth of confidence in a 2012 study.[54] It literally changes our physiology; we produce testosterone, which provides a courage boost.

❖ **Presentation** – speaking to teams and large groups with clear, simple enunciation.

❖ **Direct talk** – tackling conflict head on, being direct in response, forthright and assertive but never angry.

❖ **Calm demeanour** – staying calm, deflating negative energy of others, and leading the team through the issue when others panic or when potential failure has severe consequences.

❖ **Tone** – a calm and measured pace, assertive, authoritative, and highly personable.

❖ **Problem solving** – adopting a tried and tested method for analysing cause and effect to create a place of safety and refocus or calm the worriers.

---

[53] Amy Cuddy, *Presence: Bringing Your Boldest Self to Your Biggest Challenge*, Little, Brown and Company, 2015, Chapter 8.

[54] Cuddy, Amy J.C., Caroline A. Wilmuth and Dana Carney, 'The benefit of power posing before a high-stakes social evaluation', Harvard Business School Working Paper, No 013-027, September 2012. Available from http://nrs.harvard.edu/urn-3:HUL.InstRepos:9547823 [accessed 19 May 2022].

❖ **Humour** – skilled use of humour in crisis, taking care not to be ignorant or flippant; relaxes and motivates.

❖ **Risk management** – adopting a process for evaluating risks and consequences of success and failure. Confidence is only required when there's risk, an element of the unknown, or a gap in experience. The willingness to take controlled risks and fail is confidence. After all, nothing ventured, nothing gained. With practice and recognition that consequences are almost never life threatening, the confidence to work with managed risk can grow.

❖ **Practice** – reinforcing team confidence during practice and after every problem. Helping the team to build mental resilience and internal locus of control – personal account-ability for action and belief in their ability to do something. Real practice physically and mentally boosts confidence as it ensures we feel and memorize the experience.

Conclusion

By now we see how personal power, goal power, and process power ignite a transformation and people power makes it happen. Next we explore culture power, where the flywheel begins to turn.

Action points

1. Unlock people power; source your team for transformation and spot diverse talent and critical experience.
2. Identify and deploy to strengths and use the ABCDE method to develop performance and deal with issues.
3. Design the transformation to maximize learning; plan experiences, communication and reflection, inclusive idea development, and experiment.
4. Use technology in new and exciting ways to address information overload and make learning stick.

5. Engage the team for transformation. Create the extraordinary experience with the CIRCLE of TRUST.
6. Support wellbeing and mental health.
7. Combine great leadership and practice to build a SYMBIOTIC team and turbo boost people power.

Chapter 6

Culture power

Introduction

In this chapter we consider organizational cultures that compound the effect of goal, process, and people power to sustain transformation and high performance. First, we review leadership styles, followed by the features of a people culture, accountability culture, customer culture, and excellence culture.

Some years ago, a dynamic US logistics organization disrupted the European industry by quickly establishing itself in several countries, and scooping key contracts with large retailers. It wasn't long before my business acquired the company. I set out to understand the special sauce that had startled the competition and enthused a sceptical customer base. At first glance nothing appeared remarkable. Closer scrutiny revealed impressive operations, industry-beating safety standards, employee attitudes, tenure, attendance, and an incredible culture.

A culture for outperformance

The founding leadership created a vision, *values*, and a simple bill of rights and responsibilities for leaders and employees. They role modelled a *disciplined* focus on accountability for results, maintaining best-in-class facilities, customer focus, and people development. Every conversation focused on operational issues hindering standards, options for enhancing customer experience, and the extent to which the company was meeting its promise to support and develop people. Customer representatives were often present in the operation. Operational teams organized around customer needs

---

and actively participated in customer relationship management. Employees owned accountability, discussed standards, and enjoyed space to perform and a sense of purpose and influence. The organization was structured into only three layers. Senior leaders engaged directly with employees and resisted any temptation to add managers. This resulted in faster decision making, intimacy, an apolitical environment, and limited need for communication protocols. Prospective employees attended informal recruitment events and connected with existing employees in a two-way 'getting to know you' exercise. Interviews focused on *cultural fit* over technical expertise. New recruits attended orientation over several weeks where colleagues shared stories about how things are done, and leaders showed up every time. The focus on culture fit and leadership involvement accelerated integration, and increased retention and performance. Supervisory joiners spent a weekend away with the top leaders to fast-track alignment to the mission and connect with the top team. Early indoctrination deepened a connection with the business purpose, priorities, customer, and people focus.

Simplicity, discipline, and values-based leadership inspired employees and proved the difference between mediocrity and outperformance. Leaders in the acquiring business witnessed the power of leadership style and culture to drive results. They raised their game and transformed into a simpler business with respect for people, customers, and results.

The SPACE programme

My findings here and subsequent experience of transitions crystallized the power of culture to drive performance and the importance of five key factors, which I call the SPACE programme:

- ❖ Style of leadership is the biggest contributor to a high-performing culture.
- ❖ People respect and support encourages commitment and contribution.
- ❖ Accountable behaviour, measurement, and ownership of action and solving problems ensures disciplined deployment.
- ❖ Customer intimacy maintains purpose, prevents navel gazing, and enhances partnership.
- ❖ Excellence, an obsessive prestige mindset, pushes up standards and attracts fans.

Style of leadership

Leadership development is the first and last thing I explore before, during, and after transformation. If it isn't already clear, high-performing cultures depend on great leaders; their style and capability are critical. A review of leadership style and climate provides a window into the success attributes or shortcomings of organizational culture. My preferred tools are:

- ❖ Korn Ferry Hay Group Leadership Styles and Climate – compares a leader's style as perceived by themselves and their team, and reports the climate created by the leader.[55]
- ❖ How to Fascinate – based on the science of branding; defines top personality advantages and shows team and organizational communication style.[56]
- ❖ SPACE-related competencies – adapted to the organization. See Chapter 5.
- ❖ Employee opinion surveys.

---

[55] Korn Ferry, 'Assess: Leadership styles and climate certification'. Available from www.kornferry.com/capabilities/leadership-professional-development/training-certification/leadership-styles-and-climate [accessed 19 May 2022].
[56] How to Fascinate. Available from www.howtofascinate.com [accessed 19 May 2022].

The Korn Ferry assessment is based on reputable research conducted by Hay McBer into leadership effectiveness, which determined six distinct leadership styles:[57]

1. Directive (coercive) – demands immediate compliance: 'Do as I tell you'.
2. Visionary (authoritative) – mobilizes people towards a vision: 'Come with me'.
3. Participative (democratic) – forges consensus through participation: 'What do you think?'
4. Affiliative – creates harmony and builds emotional bonds: 'People come first'.
5. Pacesetting – sets high standards for performance: 'Do as I do, now'.
6. Coaching – develops people for the future: 'Try this'.

According to the research, each style has a distinct impact on the working atmosphere and financial performance of the organization and is least or most suited to certain situations. Leaders with the best results move fluidly between styles to fit the situation. The visionary style has the most positive impact on climate, followed closely by affiliative, participative, and coaching styles. Pacesetting works well with self-directed teams and directive styles work well in a crisis; these two styles should be used selectively.

By holding a mirror to leaders and showing how they can adapt and create the right climate, we prepare them to support transformation. Unsurprisingly, I find that analysis of any organization's leadership group reveals a dominant mix of styles, influenced by the founder's philosophy, the culture, recruitment, development, and promotion practices. The results offer guidance on personal

---

[57] Daniel Goleman, 'Leadership that gets results', *Harvard Business Review*, March–April 2000.

and group development needs. One recent organizational review revealed dominant pacesetting and directive styles in 50% of the leadership group, coupled with low people and change agility. No prizes for guessing the impact these styles were having on culture and transformation efforts.

People culture

The most frequently mentioned reasons by employees of 50 Fortune 100 companies for their company being great to work for were:[58]

- ❖ focus on performance and results;
- ❖ empowerment;
- ❖ inclusiveness;
- ❖ encouragement of authenticity;
- ❖ quality of team and team working;
- ❖ purpose and mission of the company;
- ❖ leadership approach and support;
- ❖ community focus;
- ❖ promoting diversity;
- ❖ career development and training;
- ❖ compassion;
- ❖ supporting an entrepreneurial approach.

By a mile, the best indication of a people culture or brand is the authentic voice of the employee. It's hard to imagine that any company today does not understand the importance of a people-friendly culture, yet research shows that half of employees

---

[58] Great Place to Work, '*Fortune* 100 Best Companies to Work For® 2019'. Available from www.greatplacetowork.com/best-workplaces/100-best/2019 [accessed 19 May 2022].

don't feel respected.[59] Good leaders know that to release people power you must respect and empower people, put them first in planning, involve and engage them. The most inspiring companies have great leadership and a great people brand. Starbucks' affirmation of employees as partners and advocacy for diversity and inclusion contribute to a reputation as a great employer. Salesforce express empathy when they take new employees to a homeless shelter, hospital, or public school on their first day. Netflix's unlimited vacation time and time off for new parents fulfils their people promise. In a respectful people culture, decisions include concern for people, communication is exceptional and people management practices demonstrate care and respect. Critically, such a culture also includes a commitment to performance and high standards of entry. Once on board, a person can expect challenging work and robust performance measurement.

People brand

Three things matter to employees and customers: what you do, how you do it, and what's in it for them. I am not a fan of extensive employer value propositions; the term itself is convoluted and sounds superior. I do however feel that a short powerful anthem (based on Sally Hogshead's Fascination system) that captures distinctive capability and culture forces clarity and integrity. Google's 'Work hard, play hard' conveys a clear message of what it's like to work there. One senior team I worked with, developed the anthem *Enduring Relationships, Extraordinary Results*. It offers something for all stakeholders and a checklist for what matters in the organization. Any action which does not sustain strong relationships

[59] Christine Porath, 'Half of employees don't feel respected by their bosses', *Harvard Business Review*, 19 November 2014. Available from https://hbr.org/2014/11/half-of-employees-dont-feel-respected-by-their-bosses [accessed 19 May 2022].

with employees and customers, or high-performing operations, has no place in this business.

To develop the anthem, collect feedback from employees and customers, brainstorm dominant behaviours, and decide what constitutes the distinct capability of the business. What does your company produce or do? What do customers value? When you find an anthem which resonates, it powerfully communicates the brand. A team in the same organization shaped a vivid people promise: *Outstanding Experiences, Entrepreneurial Spirit, Distinctive Careers, Talented Teams, International Adventures*. An attractive list by anyone's standards; a mix of reality and aspiration. If plausible, genuine, and backed up with action, aspiration is fine.

Features of a respectful people culture

We will now review the important characteristics of a respectful people culture: accountability; engagement; unforgettable experiences; dialogue; transition; career opportunities and personal growth; diversity; support, appreciation and recognition; and teamworking. We consider too the influence of the experience and gig economies on employee engagement.

Accountability

Accountable behaviour is an attitude and a culture in itself, which we explore in the section entitled – Accountability culture. A people culture *without accountability* is a country club and encourages rudderless and mediocre teams. An accountable culture *without respect for people* results in compliance and an unhappy, stifled workforce living in fear and protection. People like to work for companies with high standards. In fact, a company's purpose, personal empowerment, and high standards are amongst the top reasons affecting employees' desire to work for a company; work is often the primary means of satisfying our need to feel significant. It's the place where we can do something meaningful and feel valued for it.

Engagement

We all want to do a good job of work, to matter and enjoy ourselves in the process. To varying degrees we crave respect, a sense of purpose, and achievement. Some people value camaraderie, learning, recognition, and rewards; for others, the freedom to create or build a legacy are important – we want to know our efforts and sacrifices make a lasting difference. Whatever the preference, we are most engaged when these needs are met. Which means we are committed to our work and our team, we work harder, and stay longer. CLC research affirms this relationship between employee commitment, effort, and performance, showing that for every 10% improvement in commitment, there is a 6% increase in effort and a 2% uplift in performance achievement.[60] Engagement is a personal state of mind, affected by many things in the life and mind of an individual. It can change with age, family circumstances, daily interactions at work, and always depends on the quality of relationship with their manager; problems in this relationship reduce commitment, cause disengagement, and influence decisions to leave. A systemic approach to engagement is helpful when building competence and culture from a low base or to raise the bar across a large company. With experience, good leaders develop good habits, break out of compliance mode, and make engagement personal, fresh, exciting, and filled with extraordinary surprising experiences.

---

[60] Corporate Leadership Council, 'Employee engagement framework and survey', 2004.

The experience economy

There was a time when an employee might have been satisfied with a job, a fair day's pay for a fair day's work, and a few vacation days; however, employees now live in the digitally enhanced experience economy and seek something better. During the 1990s we witnessed the emergence of the experience economy. Companies differentiated by wrapping products and services within an experience. Some progressed to staging and charging for unique, memorable, and engaging experiences.[61] Walt Disney is perhaps the most recognized pioneer of the experience with his theme parks. The visitor, or more accurately guest, is immersed in a themed experience and bombarded with entertainment and escapist moments designed to connect with the Disney brand and ensure the most memorable of days. Indelible happenings take place throughout the visit – a magnificent parade, a visit to a restaurant, or an encounter with a life-sized character. Customers are distracted in long queues by props and video, which involve them in the story and neutralize negative feelings. Branded memorabilia provide associations and fuel memory of the experience long after it ends. Throughout the day, every sense is engaged, increasing pleasure and likelihood of positive recall. It doesn't take effort to understand the opportunity that exists in the experience approach in relation to engaging and retaining the best people. Companies that design significant moments increase connection, creativity, and engagement.

Unforgettable experiences

According to Chip and Dan Heath in their book *The Power of Moments*,[62] when we recall an experience, we tend to remember defining moments: the peaks – highly positive experiences like an

---

[61] Joseph Pine II and James H. Gilmore, 'Welcome to the experience economy', *Harvard Business Review*, July–August 1998.

[62] Chip and Dan Heath, *The Power of Moments: Why Certain Experiences Have Extraordinary Impact*, Penguin Random House, 2017.

exciting celebration event; the pits – unpleasant moments like a negative exchange with a colleague or boss; and the transitions – a promotion or job change. The authors describe four characteristics of a defining moment.

Elevation – a boost of sensory appeal, which raises the stakes and/or defies expectations. A training event at an unusual location, a performance challenge for the learners, or a surprise learning experience like a special visit or a virtual reality experience.

Insights – aha moments of new understanding achieved by helping people 'trip over the truth' or stretch for insight in a way they never have before. A dramatized simulation perhaps, with a coach to ask questions or offer a re-frame.

Pride – moments of recognition, milestones, or courageous moments. Using project goals or activities as celebration or awards and spontaneous moments for recognizing personal performance.

Connection – created through shared meaning and deepening of ties, bringing people together for a unifying moment focused on a meaningful activity.

Defining moments don't have to be big; they occur in the everyday environment, although by their nature they are peak rather than everyday experiences. The best moments are spontaneous, unrehearsed, and cost little. Stay alert to the possibility of elevating everyday events into peak moments and neutralizing the pits. Design experiences like meetings, conferences, and learning events. Work with the team, their participation in design may be defining in itself. Use the checklist above to ensure moments are powerful by adding elevation, insight, connection, pride, and elevation.

An unforgettable experience

At a strategy conference, presenters were charged with creating peak moments by immersing delegates in entertaining experiences. A dramatic black curtain enrobed and segregated the venue to create mysterious dens. Delegates weaved in and out unaware of what to expect. On arrival at one enclave, a movie ticket allowed entry; refreshment vendors in themed uniforms supplied popcorn and showed guests to their seats by torchlight. A short fanfare and opening titles introduced a short movie. Colleague actors role played a new process and tools, in a series of dramatic scenes. After the show the audience answered a brief recall quiz on their ticket and the winner received a prize before departing the theatre to a new memorable insight. Adoption of new processes and projects was high after the event, and the business outperformed the plan that year.

The gig economy and entrepreneur revolution

Whilst some employers have yet to grasp the idea of 'the experience' for engaging people at work, many individuals are shunning corporate life in favour of charting their own path and following their passion. From toiling to survive in the agrarian economy to struggling for basic comforts in an industrialized world. From working for a better life and career in a service economy to seeking personal growth, connection, and excitement in the experience economy, we have come full circle. Instead of working the land, people work the technology at home. They can connect with others to offer skills and services, whilst retaining independence and freedom. It takes those who choose it closer to a meaningful purpose, where the reward for hard work is in living out their potential. Wise employers recognize the choices available to talented people and work with the trend. They focus on the intangible employment proposition by creating extraordinary moments, allowing employees to channel their entrepreneurial spirit in a way which creates value for the business, and they invest in engaging remote workers.

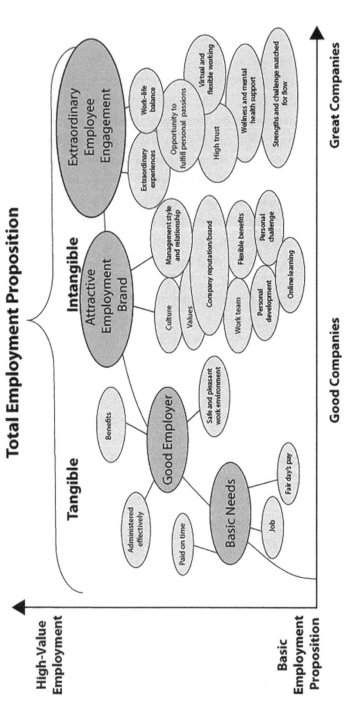

Figure 18: Extraordinary engagement

Dialogue

Communication is culture. The words we use matter; they imply authority and educate. Critically, they incite action, change people, and change the world. Careless words generate hostility and dissatisfaction. Emotional or extreme words create unnecessary drama, when simple and candid is better. When people matter, communication is crafted for precision, simplicity, and clarity. Carefully produced supporting media accelerate understanding. Recently, the world has been gripped by a global pandemic. I recall being irritated by journalists complaining of mixed messages about lockdown. I did not find the messages to be unclear; the issues seemed mostly to be sensationalized by the media or those who wanted to circumvent the rules. Each time details were clarified, another claim of confusion erupted. I wondered whether people might prefer a dictatorship, where rules are black and white and freedom to think and live is curtailed. There is certainly an argument for a more autocratic style in life-threatening crisis situations. On the other hand, in a democratic, free-speaking world where everyone has their own prejudicial interpretation, can we ever be entirely clear? What is important, however, is the dialogue, the two-way cut and thrust that provides healthy, constructive challenge, corrects misunderstandings and clarifies intentions. One-way communication without dialogue is a dictatorship. Keeping people informed and sharing decisions creates openness and stimulates healthy debate.

Culture change occurs through conversation and exposure to new thinking and new alternatives. The critical feature of dialogue is not the communicating, which occurs all too readily as we rush to fill the silence; it is the genuine listening, restating, and clarifying that create trust and understanding. Face-to-face encounters, focus groups, public and online forums, surveys, and town hall meetings encourage dialogue. Short pulse and voting surveys provide rapid access to the reactions of large groups; they enable anonymity when required and can be appended to emails and updates. Whilst tools are good for soliciting feedback, they are not a substitute for conversation and in themselves are not dialogue, unless followed up with results and focus group discussion. Impact is strongest when a short time lapses between opinion and follow-up so that employees recognize their own impact on company decisions.

Transition

Starting a new job, getting promoted, and experiencing change are highly charged moments which affect the employee's perception and experience of a company. A transition ignored is a missed opportunity for a peak moment and potentially the creation of a deep 'pit' moment. Of all the transitions, orientation or induction sets the tone of the relationship. It is the moment when an employee must receive personal attention. Transitions create anxiety, which can be converted into excitement by anticipating needs ahead of time. People are excited by a company with a mission, a supportive manager, a warm and welcoming team, and a job for which they are prepared, trained, and equipped. We give the gift of deep respect when we lead the new employee through a personalized programme, connecting them quickly with colleagues and coaching them towards a peak moment of achievement. To convert a transition into a defining moment, dissect the event to identify potential high and low points. A system of care and a supportive manager support the employee through the change.

A converted transition

Ron, a gentleman in his late 50s, faced losing the job he'd occupied for ten years. Recognizing the difficulty of a job market unfriendly to older workers, his confidence hit rock bottom. Ron's manager took up the challenge of converting the transition into a peak moment. Anticipating the inevitable, she planned a series of counselling sessions to help him re-frame the situation. Together they captured his story, highlighted experiences accrued during his career and the people he had positively impacted. With each discussion Ron grew prouder and more energized. They identified opportunities and Ron contacted former colleagues. A previous colleague remembered Ron and within days he was invited to meetings. The manager coached him in interview techniques and within two weeks he was offered two roles. Finally, she arranged a short leaving ceremony with Ron's team, acknowledged his contribution, and congratulated him. Two months after transitioning to his new role, Ron returned to thank the manager for the life-changing impact of the experience.

During change programmes, efficiencies and new methods often cause employee losses, a major source of anxiety and emotion. The approach to supporting people out of the organization sends a vital message. Increasing support leaves an enduring message with departing employees and reinforces the comfort, safety, and positivity of remaining employees. These transitions, like others, can be turned into moments of growth and progress.

Career opportunities and personal growth

Traditional fixed organizational structures and career frameworks now tend to make way for dynamic organizational design, and continuous career and development dialogue with individuals. A person-centred approach to career mapping, learning, and succession planning involves the employee and their manager in analysing experience and competence, sharing a range of future career options, and taking action to fill experience gaps and develop personal strengths. Whether structured experiences, practical application and coaching, mentoring, simulations, online workouts, or any other solution, learning is a non-negotiable investment.

Diversity

Good employers wrestle with how to resource, develop, and include teams which better reflect the diversity of society and the markets within which they operate. Diversely populated organizations with a broader representation of ethnicity, gender, or any other factor are hands down more interesting and exciting places to work. A homogeneous like-minded group work well together, share similar perspectives, and communicate easily. Such similarity, however, can result in narrow mindedness, resistance to change, and obsolescence. A diverse group may need a longer learning curve initially. Communication may be more challenging, and there's always a need for education in cultural diversity or overcoming bias. However, when companies build a diverse workforce and train teams to work together, they generate greater value. Diversity results in more innovation, faster learning, improved agility, increased attractiveness to employees and customers, and healthy profits. To create a culture in which diversity thrives, continuously role model patience, tolerance, and elimination of bias. Try my PAIR UP approach, six steps to inclusiveness.

1. People processes – form a diverse team to design prejudice out of attraction, recruitment, promotion, training, and other people processes.
2. Awareness – train in cultural awareness, inclusiveness, and recognition of own and others' bias.
3. Interrupt own patterns of bias – working with a buddy, bias check decisions, remove defensiveness, accept missteps, apologize, and correct. Check out the Harvard Implicit Association tests online.

4. **R**econcile difference – find a respectful way of working together despite differences.
5. **U**nderstand and appreciate difference – familiarise yourself with the perspectives and interests of others and appreciate the validity of their perspective.
6. **P**ractise bias-free communications – be patient, tolerant, and help others to be bias aware. Train them in how to overcome bias.

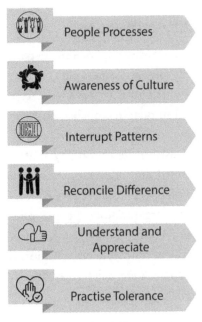

People Processes

Awareness of Culture

Interrupt Patterns

Reconcile Difference

Understand and Appreciate

Practise Tolerance

Figure 19: PAIR UP approach

Support, appreciation, and recognition

The fastest way to engage others with lasting impact is to appreciate or recognize contribution. We discussed this more fully in Chapter 5. Thoughtful feedback in recognition of a job well done is immensely powerful; it demonstrates respect, develops strengths, and makes the person feel significant and aware that their work is noticed and valued. Supporting progress in work is even more powerful. Helping people to achieve and see progress affects productivity and creativity.

Team working

We have already discussed teamworking extensively. Please refer to Chapter 5 – People power.

Accountability culture

Accountability is the answering of one person to another for results. It involves devolving business plan objectives so that people understand their contribution. Everyone is responsible for goals and tasks measured in quantity, quality, cost, and time; each has decision-making authority within the confines of their job. People are empowered to assume responsibility; initiative is rewarded, and failure is analysed and addressed. Success leads to positive consequences and failure to negative consequences. It seems simple enough; however, organizations, people, roles, and challenges are complicated. Embedding a culture takes effort and discipline. Adjusting to a highly accountable organization can be a shock to the system but if standards are well trained and consequences clarified, employees relish the structure.

Leadership

Leadership behaviour sets the tone. When leaders are disciplined and accept responsibility for their successes and mistakes, it increases trust, respect, and makes them relatable. When KFC in the UK had to close because they ran out of chicken, they owned it and placed a full-page newspaper advertisement. Customers appreciated their transparency, apology, and humour. Outside of the public eye, the consequences for the culpable supplier were swift and unequivocal.

Figure 20: KFC newspaper advertisement, 23 February 2018

To develop an accountable culture, explore strengths and weaknesses of leadership behaviour. Assess organizational processes which support or hinder accountability: communication of targets, review processes, rewards, performance management, coaching quality, and training. Train managers in good coaching habits; reinvent performance management and incentives to reward correct behaviour. Address behaviours which hinder accountability. Agree accountability beliefs and ensure leaders are prepared to model the behaviour.

Integrated business planning and review

A good review process involves timely forthright discussion on achievement or non-achievement of goals, disciplined timing and follow-up, candid discussion, dynamic presentation, and access to the support of a team for problem solving. Review processes that create industries of paperwork and effort; they are a sign of missing accountability, where people work harder to show why they fail than they work to achieve the target.

Organizational design

Some organizations are notorious for introducing new rules to solve every problem. They bury people in requests for reports, add supervisors and create inefficient structures and too many people responsible for the same decisions. The resulting role compression limits freedom to perform and causes confusion. Remove roles which don't have discrete decision-making authority. There must be clear distance between the accountability of a role and that of its superior and subordinate team. A leader must not need to take the same decisions as her team. The leader's boss must not need to encroach on her decision-making authority and must also add value to her. Interview managers. Assess their decision-making authority in terms of resources, nature of work, time frame of decisions and problem-solving activity. Where decision making is duplicated, roles can be removed, redeployed, or moved into a support capacity. Totem pole structures with deputies or confusing matrices and multiple reporting lines, signal accountability problems. To learn more, consult the Accountable Leader by Brian Dive.[63]

Accountability mindset

The holy grail of accountability is mindset: the beliefs, competence, experience, and personality which make a person comfortable with the authority to act, speak out, welcome feedback, and work hard to become expert. This mindset is founded on beliefs such as:

---

[63] Brian Dive, *The Accountable Leader: Developing Effective Leadership, Through Managerial Accountability*, Kogan Page, 2008.

I need to see an improvement from my work – overwhelming need to deliver results.

I enjoy responsibility – I want to make a difference.

Everything is not about me – I am not a victim and will not waste mental energy on stuff I can't affect.

I am candid and like it when others are – we need to say it as we see it.

I assume that I have authority – it's ok to take charge, I am free to make it happen.

I welcome feedback – I can handle it.

I own a problem – I'll take it on.

I'm not afraid to fail – I will learn.

People with an accountability mindset exhibit the following characteristics:

Results focus – ownership of action and quality work delivered on time and in budget; achieved through communication, training, a clear purpose, goals, and targets and sustained through candid performance dialogue.

Resilience – positivity, ability to overcome barriers, and seek alternative solutions. See Chapter 8. People low in resilience accept circumstances as inevitable and use this as an excuse for failing to act. They can be victims destined to complain about their lot, tell you what can't be done, and find someone else to take the responsibility.

Personal confidence – a feeling of being *capable* of doing something if they want to. Confidence comes from experience, earlier success, access to resources, and support from the boss.

Completer/finisher orientation – an obsession with finishing work. Some hard workers over-absorb workload or suffer excess perfectionism, poor time management, poor delegation, inability to say no, and a failure to insist on the contribution of others.

Team worker – able to compromise for the good of the team, without abdicating personal accountability. Performance is a team effort and everyone must complete their share of the plan. The push and pull of teamwork forces supportive behaviours. Personal accountability exists as a subset of the team goal to avoid overlap, confusion, and dropped balls.

Consequences

The idea of consequences sounds draconian, but it shouldn't be. Consequences are the internal and external rewards for good results and the sanctions for persistent failure. The reality is that most consequences tend to be positive. Luckily, achieving good results is intrinsically rewarding when capabilities are matched to the task and there's freedom to choose and fail without fear of catastrophe. Facilitate an environment of constructive accountability: recognize success, analyse problems, and coach improvement. Encourage people to speak up when they fail. Embrace it as an opportunity for everyone to learn and to boost performance. Act consistently and carefully. The team must not be afraid to act because they witness others being berated by the boss. Owning up to mistakes is not easy for most people. If they see you respond constructively to taking ownership, they will adapt.

When it comes to underperformance, some managers avoid confrontation, afraid of being seen as the bad guy. They compensate by absorbing the performance shortfall or overstretching other team members. When it all gets too much, they surprise the person with extreme consequences. Other managers relish holding people to account with frequent, humiliating challenge. The result of either style is destructive accountability, low team morale, and mediocrity. A manager must be prepared to ask difficult questions and challenge in a professional, firm, non-judgemental way, and the employee must be prepared to face up to their accountability. This tension is uncomfortable for some; discomfort is reduced by easing people into the process. When respectfully handled, people feel aware of support and respond with a healthy concern. The accountability process should allow fair and challenging discussion and enlist wider team support as appropriate. For repeated or serious failures, move to a personal improvement plan and private discussion. An accountability review requires discipline; it must happen routinely and respectfully. The objective is to energize the plan by charting progress, motivate performance through positive recognition, and facilitate accountability to the team.

The following consequence levels are a guide to help develop a natural approach, not a mechanical procedure.

Consequence level	Process
1. Being accountable to the team.	Constructive challenge is part of a team process. A familiar routine led by a professional, supportive leader should not be uncomfortable. Personal discomfort arises out of a fear of letting the side down or being the weak link. The issues and causes of failure are explored and corrective action agreed.
2. Acknowledgement of recurring failure in a team discussion.	Discussions focus on reasons for failure and a clear, time-bound commitment to remedy it. Further support from team members is agreed and the leader attends to any peripheral contributory factors.
3. Personal accountability discussion	Consistent failure is taken offline of the team and corrections are monitored. Support is provided and future consequences communicated.

4. Urgent personal performance improvement plan	Agreed time-sensitive actions. Consequences are expressed and remedial training implemented.
5. Respectful redeployment	Moving to a role where the person can be successful.

Table 2: Consequence levels

Holding others to account

Being personally accountable is tough; holding others to account is tougher. Every relationship dynamic evokes a certain action and reaction. We can be reticent about holding our bosses' toes to the fire and comfortable holding our team to account. We may feel awkward critiquing peers yet reprimand a partner or sibling without hesitation. I often come across leaders who are comfortable holding others to account and critiquing performance, but lack the humility and experience to handle personal feedback. Successful people can be insecure or inexperienced at receiving criticism. If you recognize this in yourself, develop coping skills to handle criticism without emotion and push back constructively. Your ability to receive and give feedback impacts the culture of the organization, which means you must roll with the punches and be able to withstand harsh and potentially unfair judgement at times. Role playing your response to difficult feedback develops a thicker skin. What's the worst feedback you could receive? What emotion does this evoke? Why does this hurt so much? Are you being honest with yourself? This self-awareness is the foundation on which to build the correct techniques for holding others accountable. It's a process of enquiry without inferring negative motives, evaluation without passing judgement, and correction planning by agreement. The skills include assertiveness to broach the discussion, verbal mastery in selecting constructive words, empathy for choosing a tone that will elicit the right response, and diplomacy to deal with conflict or emotion.

Assertive interactions

Accountability discussions are opportunities for positive recognition and progress chasing. Inevitably, issues and performance shortfalls are highlighted and require attention. Handling performance issues can create anxiety for leaders and the team. An assertive interaction tackles performance with clarity and empathy through a clear request for change and a commitment to work together on a solution. To build confidence in assertive interactions I train leaders in the DESIRED performance routine.

After questioning and evaluation:

1. **D**escribe the observed failure (or success), the repeated performance shortfall, and its components, being as specific as possible. The person should not have to 'read the tea leaves' or guess the meaning. Coaching discussions provide opportunity to develop ideas and agree on the specific options.
2. **E**mpathize. Understand the intention; look beneath the performance problem. Whilst their efforts may not have been successful, they are well intentioned. Express appreciation and understanding to reduce defensiveness. Be supportive.
3. **S**upport positive efforts and results, however limited. Acknowledge their efforts to minimize anxiety and encourage focus on the way forward.
4. **I**mpact. Describe the effects of the failure on others, including their feelings, e.g., frustration, discomfort, strain, anxiety. People do not like to be responsible for the discomfort of others. When explained, it can jolt a person to act.

5. Request a new outcome. The person may need guidance.
6. Empower the person to choose their course of action and retain accountability.
7. Discuss and compromise – work together to find a solution which works for both parties.

Team accountability review – Part 1

Sam is leading his team through the weekly accountability hour. The teams are standing around boards which display the new business implementation objectives and current performance progress.

Sam: Ok team let's get down to business; we've got a lot to get through. Jane, can you lead us through your objectives? In the interests of time please keep to the brief highlights of completed actions; I want us to focus on the actions currently in the *red*.

Jane: No problem. First, action item 2.0: Completed Risk Assessments. All implementation risk assessments have been completed and recorded. We faced a few challenges with availability of key people but managed to pull in the final couple on Monday. A few critical issues have been identified; owners now have the risk assessments and are action planning mitigation activities.

Sam: Yes, I noticed the risks identified around the production plan and the swift response. That was well spotted by your team; it could have easily been missed. Please thank the team for their attentiveness.

Jane: I will, thank you. Item 2.2 is the compilation of the resourcing plan. Unfortunately, this is running behind schedule, but we think we will be back on target in the next two weeks.

Sam: That's a real concern Jane; we have six weeks to get teams recruited and trained. What's caused the problem?

Jane: It's basically the absence of a team member and I had to divert people into solving emergency production issues.

Sam: I recognize the production challenge. Given the sensitivity of this resourcing plan and the interdependencies we need this to be done sooner. What can you do to put it right?

Simon: I can spare a couple of people for three days to pick up the production issues.

Jane: Thanks, that will help a lot. I'll re-prioritize a couple of tasks and make sure we get back on track.

Sam: We need a firm and final date for the plan.

Jane: I will circulate a final plan and initiate all recruiting by next week's meeting.

Sam: Ok Jane, can you record this new time commitment on the board; please make sure the plan is complete and call on the rest of the team if you need help. It won't be acceptable to exceed this new time frame.

> Jane: Sure, I will just need a commitment from each of the team to make time to sign off on the plan by Friday.
>
> Sam: I will make sure I do this, can everyone agree? He gestures around collecting an affirmative response from every person.

Each team member accounts for their actions in the presence of the team. The leader recognizes achievement by showing he noticed something and thanking them. He explores the failure and requests action to get back on course. The owner is asked to commit in front of the team. The leader reciprocates with public commitment and requests the team do the same. The likelihood of compliance and achievement when we make a public commitment is greatly increased because of our innate need to feel consistent. See Robert Cialdini's work – *Influence*.[64] When we write it down and make the commitment without undue external pressure it strengthens our commitment. Jane was merely asked to improve the situation; however, she applied a demanding timeline and extended the goal to include other actions.

Team accountability review – Part 2

> Sam: Ok Martin, can you talk us through your objectives please?
>
> Martin: I need to update you on product design. We are struggling to achieve the specification the customer requested. There's a supply issue on several components. We've tried to resolve it, but suppliers aren't

---

[64] Robert Cialdini, *Influence: The Psychology of Persuasion*, HarperCollins, 2007.

cooperating, and the customer keeps changing the goal posts with adjustments.

Sam: Thanks for your candour. I know there have been efforts to address the problem and I have supported the actions you have taken so far; unfortunately, the approach is not working. I am concerned about the pace and absence of a clear solution. I know some in the team are frustrated; they are experiencing additional work because of the delays and inter-dependencies with their activities. Let's capture your immediate action plan now and follow up in a 30-minute problem-solving discussion with interested parties later today. We must get this design up to specification.

The seriousness of repeated failure is acknowledged with the team and corrective action sought. If failure persists, consequence level three takes the discussion offline of the team. When a performance explanation is inadequate, the leader must make this clear. Holding back diminishes the gravity of the situation and frustrates the team. Disappointment is expressed in a respectful manner, ensuring the recipient grows concerned whilst retaining dignity. It's possible to appreciate efforts and comment on good progress, whilst showing dissatisfaction with outcome and the negative impact on others. Maintaining the integrity of the accountability session is important for brevity and focus; problem solving happens in a separate session with the support of the team. Tone is important: people need to know the boundaries of acceptability; however, it's not appropriate or productive to levy personal or humiliating criticism in public.

Coaching for accountability

Coaching is an important tool supporting accountability. See the 'A' GAME ON process described in Chapter 4.

Customer culture

Attracting and retaining customers is more challenging than ever before because tastes and expectations have been revolutionized by the influence of technology on daily life. Products and services commoditize fast, barriers to market entry disappear overnight, and market disruptors spring out of nowhere. To stay relevant a business must adapt to trends, align plans with the customers', create intimacy, and design and personalize experiences which bond. Such a customer-focused culture has distinct features: leaders who walk the talk and serve their employees first, in the knowledge that they will reciprocate with service to the customers; happy employees selected for their customer empathy, who are well trained and work closely with and for customers; and a philosophy of enhancing the customer experience, innovating for the benefit of the customer and personalizing service.

Leadership excellence = Employee engagement and accountability = Customer engagement

We know that what leaders say, do, and reward influences the behaviour and commitment of the team. When leaders who are highly visible demonstrate integrity and a caring, nurturing, and empowering style, employees reciprocate in their attitude to work. Research conducted by David Ulrich, Professor of Business at the Ross School of Business in Michigan suggests that, for every 10% increase in engagement levels, a company's customer service levels go up by 5% and profits by 2%.[65]

---

[65] Spearhead Training, 'Leadership and engagement'. Available from www.spearhead-training.co.uk/blog/leadership-and-engagement [accessed 19 May 2022].

❖ Build belief in the brand. Employees who feel proud of their mission and understand how their work impacts the customer, develop a deeper sense of responsibility and service. When radiologists were shown photos of the patients whose X-rays they were scanning, they increased both the raw number and accuracy of their scans. When nurses assembling surgical kits met a caregiver who would use the kits, they worked 64% longer than a control group and made 15% fewer errors.[66]

❖ Recognize people for the small things that make a difference to the customer. Encourage peer-to-peer recognition of customer care. Notice everything and help people whose actions are remote or indirect to see their impact on the customer. Take care not to limit recognition to those who work directly with customers.

❖ Create emotional connection by ensuring people see and interact with a customer. Arrange events or situations where employees can interact with customers and increase feelings of commitment.

❖ Sponsor an experience focus – continuously revisit the customer experience; engage the teams in working with customers to improve touch points and redesign the customer experience.

❖ Obsessively respond to customers. Demonstrate responsiveness to employees and demand they do the same with customers. Measure and track responsiveness.

❖ Strengthen the team's sense of purpose by showing how simple things change the customer experience and emphasizing connections to customers.

---

[66] Chip and Dan Heath, *The Power of Moments: Why Certain Experiences Have Extraordinary Impact*, Penguin Random House, 2017, p. 219.

Employee engagement and accountability = Customer engagement

People with a service attitude build a service culture. Seek out people with a passion for great service, those who demonstrate awareness of their customers and embody company values. Prioritize the comfort and happiness of new employees and introduce customers early – who they are, their expectations, and how they are being met. Bring the customer to life through technology or real-life presence. Show people how to connect with customers and build relationships, examine every customer interface, highlight great service, and show how a service attitude is rewarded. Provide training and tools for solving customer issues. Discuss extraordinary service and pose challenges which develop a service attitude.

The customer experience

Customers are no longer content to buy a quality product and service, they thirst for the experience. Millennials are four times more prepared to spend on an experience than physical goods, according to a report by McKinsey.[67] With a smart phone and camera in hand, they mean to make every minute count. Other generations have picked up the baton too – an instant social media update on an event, a show, or extravagant meal creates experience envy. Brands that create the experience understand how to connect with the customer on an emotional level by provoking sensory engagement and a sense of pride or achievement. Research by McKinsey showed that improving a customer

---

[67] Bo Finneman, Julia Ivory, Sophie Marchessou, Jennifer Schmidt, and Tom Skiles, 'Cracking the code on millennial consumers', McKinsey & Company, 18 March 2017. Available from www.mckinsey.com/industries/retail/our-insights/cracking-the-code-on-millennial-consumers [accessed 19 May 2022].

experience from average to exceptional (where the customer is 'wowed' in some way) can lead to a 30 to 50% increase in indicators such as likelihood to renew or purchase another product. The customer experience begins with the extraordinary employee experience. Work with the team to evaluate, enhance, and personalize every customer touch point: the aesthetics of the experience, the people they interact with in the organization, the processes, the service technology, the product, the place they attend, and the price they pay. Consider how this matches styles and meets customer needs.[68]

Customer intimacy

Cruising a highway along the Arabian Gulf, on the way to our hotel, my husband and I suspected something might be different when we caught sight of a majestic structure. As we pulled up, the door sprung open. An informal, authoritative young man thrust out a hand, greeted us by name, and politely whisked us through a stunning entrance hall. We transitioned seamlessly through an invisible check-in process and within moments were riding the lift. Feeling impressed with the personalized, efficient reception and the smart room, we stepped outside. A breath-taking view, across a palm-bordered poolside, over the bay to the iconic Jumeirah skyline, was etched on our memory. Every experience thereafter surpassed expectation. Beneath the fabric of this glossy hotel flourished something much more remarkable than beautiful surroundings. An extraordinary service culture. Day after day we were greeted with authentic

---

[68] Dorian Stone and Joel Maynes, 'For customer loyalty, only the best will do', McKinsey & Company, 1 February 2014. Available from www.mckinsey.com/business-functions/growth-marketing-and-sales/our-insights/for-customer-loyalty-only-the-best-will-do [accessed 19 May 2022].

personal attention where names were memorized and preferences anticipated. Every interaction included a twist. Staff appeared to assist at appropriate moments, stopping briefly for a chat. When our stay was interrupted with disturbance, security personnel acted expediently and most surprisingly; the staff we encountered later were aware and compensated with small service gestures. At departure the check-out clerk volunteered the deduction of a night's stay from the bill and the manager manifested suddenly to inquire about our stay.

This seemingly effortless service did not exist by chance or procedures alone. The hotel installed a culture of customer experience, underpinned by careful selection, training, engagement of teams, and the mindful design of every guest interaction. Without this, the event would have been a stay not an experience, generic rather than personalized, and forgettable rather than memorable. The skilled team, empowered to create exceptional experience, seeded a memorable experience, creating a lifelong connection with this business. From our discussions, it seemed that staff were selected for their relationship skills, trained to offer and continuously improve a great guest experience, and rewarded for doing so. They felt it was their responsibility to connect with guests and solve problems. Each person described a long-term career plan and great opportunities provided by the company.

The personalization edge

A great experience is the new normal; however, what's exciting for one person may be mildly interesting to another. The competitive edge lies in personalizing the experience as far as possible. Customers enjoy the reliability of standard, but they also want something tailored that others don't have. Big data and artificial intelligence have opened the door to scalable personalization by allowing insight into the lives and purchasing preferences of consumers. Pop-up advertising spookily reflects our latest interest; a retailer discount lands in the inbox at the perfect moment. Whilst customers love intuitive technology and a seamless experience, a very real moment of human interaction and personal attention, acknowledgement has the winning edge.

To personalize the experience, revisit the core tenets of good customer service and add a twist.

- ❖ Check the technology interface, making sure the experience is seamless, enjoyable, and creates a unique web experience. Amazon is the leader in this space, offering suggestions based on previous history.
- ❖ Engage the team in hunting down personalization opportunities throughout the customer journey. Carefully choreograph moments, communicate between departments to pass on insights, and make the customer feel special with a proactive gesture.
- ❖ Know the customer – collect and analyse data. Account managers and other relationship owners are crucial sources of knowledge on customer's styles, preferences, expectations, and their current experience with your business.
- ❖ Empower the team to act spontaneously; trust them with total freedom or provide broad parameters within which they can serve the customer.
- ❖ Know the customer by name – there's a reason Starbucks and other service companies use a customer's first name. Our brains work differently when we hear our name, a scientifically evidenced fact; we tune in when we hear it, and we tune out other noise.
- ❖ Recognize and reward loyal customers with small gestures. Marks & Spencer, a British retailer, use their Sparks programme to reward regular shoppers with a small gift and regular discounts.

- ❖ Sponsor events for VIPs providing early access, special discounts, or other perks. Make the experience memorable.
- ❖ Send handwritten notes. Overuse of technology to communicate becomes impersonal. Personal communications which don't rely on automation can be more meaningful. Maintain certain efficient automated routines and design out obvious robotic features.
- ❖ Ask for feedback on areas for improvement; listen and personalize response. When feedback is accepted, it increases feelings of significance, respect, and loyalty. A failure to listen and ignored concerns repel; according to research 68% of consumers abandon a business because they feel the brand does not care about them.[69] There are many ways to hear the voice of the customer: commissioned surveys, account management discussions, industry events, direct solicitation, and real-time reactions.

Customer intimacy

When employees feel a sense of service and accountability to the customer, the company enjoys strong, trusting customer relationships and is easy to do business with. Closeness is difficult in larger organizations with complexity and management layers. Limit the levels of accountability between the top of the organization and the customer. Nordstrom, a large US retailer famous for customer service, describes the organization as an inverted pyramid. Customers are at the top; sales, support, and operational people at the next level; then managers and executives. Everyone spends time in the roles directly below the customer to instil knowledge

---

[69] Atif M., 'Reinventing personalization for customer experience: Why? What? How?', Towards Data Science, 30 May 2019. Available from https://towardsdatascience.com/reinventing-personalization-for-customer-experience-235d8c75aa38 [accessed 19 May 2022].

of the front-line experience, a sense of serving, and appreciation of what it takes to satisfy a customer.

Job titles emphasize culture and imply customer intimacy. They are emotive symbols of status, so messing with them can be tricky. There's high symbolic value and cultural effect when titles connect with the customer and maintain significance for the role holder. Some IT organizations have taken the lead from Apple and call their IT service engineers and retail staff Genius, Creative Pros, and other names denoting expertise levels. The Make a Wish Foundation empowered employees to create whimsical and meaningful role titles illustrating their values, talents, and contributions. The Chief Operating Officer became the Minister of Dollars and Sense, whilst the Administrative Assistant became the Goddess of Greetings.

Ask employees to work out what they do for the customer. Help them follow the effect of their actions to find a meaningful title or a personal brand statement to increase customer connection by triggering curiosity and conversations. When organizational barriers to intimacy are removed, focus can shift to improving the experience, increasing the frequency and quality of interactions, and empowering employees to serve the customer.

Irresistible quality

Customer intimacy cannot be achieved without quality products and excellent service. We would never accept perished food from the store or book a flight with a company that reached the destination occasionally. Unfortunately, our demand for 100% quality does not always carry over into the way we do our work. Organizations overcome the challenge of maintaining quality with strict standards, methodical systems, measurement, defect management, and continuous improvement, but this is only the beginning. Irresistible quality is an attitude and a culture which transcends process; it's a passion which starts with leadership and is reinforced through behaviour at every stage of the building, testing, and sale of goods. When the leader refuses to accept mediocrity, the organization follows suit. See 'Excellence culture' below.

Innovation and reinvention

Disruptive innovation by left-field insurgents creates many a lost customer. Established business suffers at the hands of new market entrants, armed with a new technology or a counterintuitive approach. The antidote is innovation and a willingness to constantly reinvent before the peak of the performance curve. Innovation is the source of competitive advantage and higher profits that business seeks. Identify ways to interconnect your business with the customers through joint decision making and making innovative tweaks to the customer experience and the product. Make innovation values central to customer service and make it safe for people to innovate. Reward successful innovation. A customer intimacy programme in one business involved the use of a joint business planning process to improve customer needs analysis and access to innovation. 80% of customers in the programme scored positive in satisfaction and loyalty compared with only 35% in the non-enrolled group. During an 18-month period, 65% of enrolled customers reported improved satisfaction through exposure to innovation, whilst 43% of the non-enrolled group became less satisfied over the same period.

Excellence culture

Excellence is an attitude, an obsession, and a deep aversion to mediocrity. If I've done my job properly, you will have concluded that a culture of excellence is the product of all that we have discussed so far: goal power, a great vision with high expectations; the discipline, rigour, and change management of process power; the engagement and commitment created by people power; and the combination of great leadership, and a people, accountability, and customer culture. Additionally, however, excellence is predicated on the existence of a quality management system: policies, philosophies, and quality objectives backed by a formalized system that documents processes, procedures, and responsibilities for assuring quality.

A quality management system

During my early career, I implemented a Total Quality Management approach in a service company. We trained leaders and teams, and deployed disciplined procedures, defect identification, complaint management systems, and continuous improvement methods. Implementation was difficult and bureaucratic; however, the business undoubtedly improved. We were rewarded with the ISO standard. Systems operated well, people complied with procedures, and damage and waste declined. Eighteen months in, some departments experienced strong results whilst others did not. A team set about studying the characteristics of the successful teams and their comparators. The following five success factors were identified in relation to the best teams:

Topflight teams	Mediocre teams
Hands-on leadership	*Distracted leadership*
Leaders discussed plans and targets daily, walked the floor, engaged in conflict handling and problem solving, and reinforced standards. Team members recounted leadership attitudes and their influential stories.	Leaders displayed conflicting priorities, were intermittently present and less focused on quality.

Small, empowered teams	Disparate teams
Teams consisted of fewer people who had been together longer and enjoyed strong camaraderie, a sense of responsibility to each other, and concern for results. They assumed authority for problems and collaborated to find the right solution.	Teams were larger, inwardly focused with evidence of cliques and conflict. They struggled with admitting defects or problems. Membership changed and colleagues were at different stages of maturity, sometimes pulling in different directions.
Passionate values and mission	Scepticism and minimalism
Teams connected strongly with the idea of world-class service, quality, and excellence. An ambition to be high performing and a preoccupation with zero errors generated frank discussions and occasional conflicts.	Teams exhibited neutral or negative mindset and mixed enthusiasm. The quality systems and focus were perceived as extra work, non-value adding, or less important than other priorities.
Simple measurement and tracking habits	Undisciplined routines
Teams held a clear idea of how to win. They identified a small number of key metrics and, in some cases, a single measure to guide action. They shared the habit of checking the simple daily metrics.	Teams employed compliance-driven routines and used measurement, tracking, and briefing inconsistently.

Training and team building	Basic training
Each team engaged in team-building activity. Leaders refreshed and re-energized training and deployed an effective new employee orientation.	Leaders delivered good initial training, although with limited follow-up and refresh.

Table 3: Success factors of topflight and mediocre teams

These five principles can be seen in other examples of successful quality systems, like McDonald's, for example, founded by Ray Kroc.

Excellence and a transformation superhero

Ray Kroc, founder of McDonald's, and author of *Grinding It Out* was 52 when he spotted the opportunity to create the world's most successful fast-food restaurant. He had, up to this point, acquired a lifetime's knowledge and experience, which coalesced into razor-sharp intuition, conviction, and a capacity to act on his instincts when it mattered most.

During a visit to a restaurant in San Bernardino, California, he seized upon a unique system painstakingly designed by the McDonald Brothers, which enabled high volume and instant service of consistently good-quality food. He replicated the system, first nationwide then internationally, turning the business into a franchised real estate and operating model. At the time of his death 7,500 outlets operated in the United States and 31 other territories. We now know McDonald's as the largest fast-food chain in the world, reputed for excellence and quality. His achievement can appear deceptively easy, yet many who followed underperformed in comparison. He took the 'Speedy Service System', the McDonald's name, the symbol of the Golden Arches, and combined it with the vision of a family restaurant. He added astute marketing, a product quality obsession, and his three pillars of decision making: employees, customers, and suppliers.

Ray standardized methods, hand-picked suppliers, and set strict franchisee rules on food supply, manufacture, portion size, cooking methods, times, and packaging. Fanatical about efficiency, speed of the system, ensuring zero process waste, and maintaining value through a limited menu, he refused cost-cutting measures that would impact taste and introduced refund penalties if customers waited too long for food. Ray personally recruited the franchisees, indoctrinated them with his principles, and contracted them to strict adherence. He also empowered and collaborated with them in the interests of continuous improvement, adapting menus on their recommendation. Success was no walk in the park; it did not come until he discovered, through collaboration with his colleague Harry Sonneborn, that real wealth could be generated by owning the restaurant real estate.

Ray Kroc and the McDonald Brothers were ahead of their time. The TQM philosophy was embryonic at the time; it went on to be developed further in Japan by William E. Deming. Kaizen ('Change for Better') continuous improvement methodology and Lean Manufacturing, with its goals of improving quality, eliminating waste, reducing process time, and reducing costs, came later. Six Sigma techniques emerged in the 1980s, providing methods and statistical tools for process control.

Embedding excellence

The McDonald's story is amongst the best examples of an obsessive founder's vision, reinforced through hands-on leadership, and careful selection of a culturally attuned supporting team. The franchise ownership model meant leaders had 'skin in the game' from day one and were licensed to use the standard operating model. Discrete locations facilitated small tight teams working near their leaders; locally empowered, yet globally standard, they focused on simple, highly visible performance metrics. His clear mission and values resonated and engaged people to the cause, whilst his value of equal respect for employees, customers, and suppliers engendered commitment to deliver.

Sustaining excellence

When entrepreneurs start up, they work with a small, specially selected group of energetic people aligned to their mission; contagious passions and values are reinforced through a personal connection with the entrepreneur. As the business grows it becomes difficult to maintain the same evangelism. Adaptations are made, which sap the initial energy. Employees yearn to recover the excitement of the early days; they collect baggage and attach to history. As more people join, diverse styles and competence dilute the culture. This is how well-intended organizations lose focus on excellence, and why large complex organizations struggle to adopt a culture widely. McDonald's sustained the model despite ever-increasing size through:

- ❖ a simple mission of customer value and excellent quality that everyone can relate to;
- ❖ a consistent, disciplined system of supply and operation;
- ❖ a tight, limited focus and unwillingness to dilute effort;

- ❖ continual improvement and enhancement;
- ❖ small, tight-knit, empowered teams;
- ❖ hands-on leadership by people with a strong interest in winning and meeting high standards;
- ❖ good training;
- ❖ simple and visible performance criteria.

An effective quality management system, the five factors of topflight teams: hands-on leadership, small, empowered teams, passionate values and mission, simple measurement and tracking, training and team building, and the following cultural practices lead to irresistible quality and excellence:

- ❖ prioritized customer experience and customer value;
- ❖ recruitment for cultural fit;
- ❖ early and continuous training;
- ❖ team building;
- ❖ quality and excellence values and continuous improvement, embedded in behaviour;
- ❖ systems, optimization, and flow – the team understand the importance of process and continuously optimize flow;
- ❖ high satisfaction – talented people and their passions are matched with roles;
- ❖ teams are tight, empowered, and collaborative;
- ❖ clear accountability through simple measures and disciplined behaviours.

In summary, a culture of excellence is inherent in a business that has a people, accountability, and customer culture. An effective quality management system, hands-on leadership with a driving passion for excellence, and small empowered teams are the different aspects that make the difference.

Conclusion

In this chapter, we have explored four cultures as if they are distinct. In reality, culture is always multi-layered. The goal must be to develop a unified SPACE culture: Styles (of leadership), People, Accountability, Customer, and Excellence. When this culture exists, transformation accelerates, and the flywheel begins to turn with ever-increasing benefits. Let's now explore the use of smart power for supporting that momentum and sustaining the benefits of transformation for the long term.

Action points

1. Compare your organization with the five components of the SPACE programme.
2. Assess the current culture, exploring leadership behaviours and practices.
3. Create an extraordinary employee experience through dialogue and defining moments.
4. Invest in small beautiful, diverse teams focused on irresistible quality and customer value.
5. Build an accountable mindset and train techniques for maintaining accountability.
6. Embed the customer experience in the employee experience; build brand belief.
7. Enhance the customer experience, add a service twist, and gain the personalization and intimacy edge.

Chapter 7

Smart power

Introduction

Power is the capacity to influence others; according to the political scientist Joseph Nye, it can be *hard*, *soft*, and *smart*. He describes soft power as a unique source of influence that countries can use to persuade or attract others to do things their way, or to move in their direction.[70] Its seductive influence is achieved through culture, history, ideology, and institutions. When a country's culture, political policies, and ideals are seen as legitimate in the eyes of others, soft power is enhanced. This contrasts with hard power, which is exercised through coercion, threat, and payment. In the political sphere this translates to military and economic power. The fall of the Berlin Wall, for example, happened *not* in response to hard power and military threats, but because of the soft power of political communication and symbols of western culture displayed in the media and entertainment. People in the Eastern Bloc, disenfranchised with the restraint of communism, were attracted to a different way of life, through a persistent and multifaceted campaign by the west to share democratic values. Smart power is the careful application of both soft and hard power, contingent upon the context and the players involved.

In this chapter we explore the importance of influence in transformation. We look briefly at hard power and sources of power in organizations. We go on to consider the selective use of hard power during transformation and ultimately spend more time on the strategies of soft power as the core means for winning hearts and minds.

---

[70] Joseph S. Nye, *Soft Power: The Means to Success in World Politics*, Public Affairs, 2004, p. 100.

Smart power in action

Business transformation is a game of influence; it begins with selling an idea for change in which the risks, investments, and costs of disruption are considerable. Powerful characters must be persuaded to hand over the crown jewels. To make progress, a coalition is required at multiple levels or paralysis sets in. The impact of the planned transformation on organizational structures and power bases contributes to support or resistance. And as if senior buy-in is not challenging enough, the hard work then begins with securing support from managers and employees, who truly hold the power to make change happen. It's possible to get their attention with autocratic decision making and a demand for compliance; the threat of losing a job or status can compel most people to do as asked. The result, however, is superficial. Resentment, rebellion, and subterfuge develop. Any positive effect is shortlived. Conversely, when persuaded through the power of consultation, education, and positive example, the hearts and minds of employees are engaged, and their personal values reinforced or adjusted to fit the new paradigm. Results may take longer to achieve but they are strong and sustainable. Transformation involves changing attitudes and habits, the achievement of which depends upon a high degree of belief in the approach or ideology. Soft power, yielded over time, is therefore the most effective and sustainable approach to influence, in combination with the use of shared power and very selective hints of hard power.

Hard power

When organization leaders impose autocratic decisions through the formal power provided by their role, or when they create consequences through the selective use of rewards and penalties, hard power is in play. Soft power is in play through more subtle means. The transformation leader has several influences at their disposal:

the authority conferred by their appointment to the role and the use of rewards and penalties; the referent authority from their association with senior people who support the direction of the plan; the expert power afforded by their valuable scarce skills which add weight to their opinion; the informational power gained through access to privileged information; the resource power from access to investment funds and their team. This leader also has the charisma power provided by their personality and reputation, if liked or respected for their approach, and the benefit of a wide range of soft power sources, which we will explore shortly.

Selective hard power

Classical management theories influenced the development of organizations, the distribution of work, and the establishment of legitimate and formal power afforded by seniority. These influences are alive and kicking today in hierarchical organizations with functions or technical departments and in some leaders who employ command and control directive styles. That said, modern thinking and experience is increasingly proving the beneficial impact of a human relations approach, the application of systems thinking, and a more transformational style of leadership in increasing effectiveness, achieving results and a flexible, resilient organization.

Transformation involves attracting people to a new way of working and persuading them to change belief and adopt an updated mindset. It's always possible to insist that people act a certain way, although their commitment is not sustainable until they are persuaded and truly convinced. Occasionally, hard power is used selectively to demand compliance or direct a behaviour. This is followed swiftly by the soft power of consultation, communication, and marketing. The individual may initially be resistant and develop a new attitude only after experiencing the positive effects of the new way of working. See the example in the next case study.

Experience changes attitude

Following a merger of two companies, top leadership decided to implement a unified performance management process to help integrate the workforce. Resistance was high; to incoming teams this was a symbol of takeover. Peter, a manager typical of the affected group, reacts, 'We really don't need this now; my team work well with our existing framework. It will take forever to convert at a time when we're making real progress'. Various methods of communication sold the new procedure and its benefits. Dissent and discontent remained. Finally, the implementation timetable arrived and managers like Peter and their teams were trained. 'It's clunky; I can barely get my head around it, never mind how difficult it will be for the team. How am I expected to deliver results when I have this to contend with?' The deployment timetable was clear and managers knew the consequences for failing to act. Pay awards and incentives would not be processed for employees whose review was not completed. Reluctantly, leaders adopted the process, the new competency model, and the supporting workflow.

When the process was complete, Peter commented on his experience. 'It wasn't that bad really; I liked the system, it forced input from my team ahead of the meeting. It was more organized.' Support and motivation grew after the first exercise, as managers enjoyed the effect on relationships and the continued data visibility. After a second cycle, attitudes were largely positive. The process was further simplified and many users became converts.

This display of hard power involved a reasonable requirement to comply, a non-draconian expectation. Consequences were appropriate and uncomfortable, without being extreme. Resorting too regularly to a directive strategy would negatively impact the work climate. In this scenario however, teams had to be pushed to experience the emotion of success to be convinced.

Soft power

Transformation is a test of winning hearts and minds; strategic use of soft power breaks down resistance and attracts supporters and participants. It can be applied through the selling process and built over time through culture and values. Power is soft because of the understated way in which it nudges and does not force or threaten. The more infiltrated and invisible it is in daily life, the more effective it becomes. Subtle undertones turn into power when unconscious bias develops in the way people think and act. A single source of influence may be strong, but influence becomes soft power when it is widely spread through culture, values, and practices. For example, a department with consistently phenomenal results builds up a bank of soft power without having to do anything else. If performance wanes however, power disintegrates in the absence of other soft power influences.

Soft power is subjective; it works because we are drawn to success, and migrate towards people like us or those who share our views. We're attracted to physical appearance or aesthetics, and we buy in to ideologies and things we like. The same factors that make us like one idea or person can equally result in dislike. The effect of soft power on transformation is not to be underestimated or left to chance. Consider soft power strategies as an important influence; however, be aware that soft power can also repel as much as it can attract. Think about the ways in which transformation can attract and repel stakeholder groups and influential people. Existing culture and policies have soft power which must be built upon or substituted as necessary.

Soft power strategies
Vision and values

A strong vision has a self-regulating effect on the behaviour of an audience; it connects the now with the future and is the epitome of soft power. We explored the power of the vision in Chapter 3. It invites the audience to participate, meets unmet needs, addresses threats, and promises success, self-esteem, and a hint of making the impossible possible. Followers are mesmerized by a credible leader who espouses and lives by a vision and ideology and is prepared to defend it at all costs; they align with this vision and act in support. Understand the soft power potential of the vision. Be clear about underpinning beliefs, values and ideology, and the needs you are meeting for your audience. Paint a picture of the future state and invite others to connect and build on the vision.

Reputation and credibility

Power is inferred in high-performing teams. A team with a history of fulfilling goals or delivering and supporting change attract attention, support, and investment. A consistent performance establishes authority: 'this team know their stuff'. Most teams have some credibility or they don't exist for long, although some have a mixed reputation. A human resources department may enjoy strong relationships with business partners because of high-quality service and expertise. Their ability for strategic impact, however, may be limited by a failure to modernize or measure performance because of outdated technology.

When planning an ambitious programme, maintain and enhance a strong image within the organization because soft power is built over time. Positive reputation is amplified through demonstrating consistent performance, relevance, and integrity in dealings and relationships. Commit to a goal, deliver, and remind stakeholders of progress. Support other teams and follow through on commitments.

Contribute beyond the scope of the team's immediate role. Update on progress in briefings and communications, build high-quality communication materials to support. Include updates in daily discussions. Educate the team to describe achievements professionally and sensitively. Marketing of achievements is not justification of one's existence, it is necessary in a world where many voices and information feeds compete for scarce attention.

Disciples and evangelists

Disciples and a few evangelists are important weapons of soft power. We know already the importance of crafted communications, imagery, and metaphors in converting people into believers. Develop positive, supportive, and collaborative relationships and co-opt people from other teams. Recruiting contributions into the team provides fresh perspectives during challenging times and builds loyalty and outward influence. Whether they have formal or informal responsibility to support the team, ensure they are involved in meetings, consulted over changes, and included in team-building activities to increase their sense of belonging. Acknowledge and reward their contribution and efforts; treat them with respect, equality, and empathy. Giving people a say in matters they would not normally influence increases feelings of significance; they become part of the support group and assume responsibility for its success.

Evangelists are created when an individual enjoys fantastic experiences with the team, when they see alignment, and are included in building plans. They reinforce the programme objectives in different settings and alter the course of negative conversations in other teams. They become vocal persuaders and supporters, convincing the naysayers to an improved understanding. In rare cases, detractors are converted to evangelists and can be the most effective influencers in the camp. See Prisoners in Chapter 4.

Prisoner turned super player

A senior leader, respected for her knowledge and commercial aptitude, routinely complained about and disparaged a transformation programme to sceptical senior colleagues. She courted like-minded individuals and created distraction. By deliberate design, she was amongst the first to feel the benefit of the changes, which made her life easier in several ways. Within a few weeks she declared her mistake, changed approach, and recounted her positive experience in several forums. The conversion from her usual pessimistic personality to a positive supporter made her compliments more noticeable and boosted the programme image. The sceptical or 'fence sitting' managers converted quicker and transformation accelerated.

Stakeholder needs

Support is generated through listening to concerns and understanding and addressing needs. To the extent that it is possible, the inclusion of stakeholders in vision development, design, and implementation improves commitment and increases willingness to engage constructively with the plan. One size never fits all; follow up and respond to individual concerns to build respect. It's dangerous to assume stakeholders are aware of the ways in which their interests and feedback have been accommodated. Make changes or choices arising out of stakeholder needs highly visible.

External and internal customers

Customers can be particularly influential and their engagement can be sought in several ways. Communicate the transformation to create a competitive edge, highlighting expertise and innovation. Professionally organize and conduct communication; package the programme coherently to attract their interest. An invitation to attend a workshop about a state-of-the-art transformation provides the customer with a personal development opportunity.

Feedback surveys and workshops improve connections with customers so long as there is visible follow-up action. It may seem inappropriate to seek customer feedback on internal matters; however, customer companies or groups always include experts who can be obliging sources of experience. Work closely with the sales team in your own organization to manage the process. This often means engaging with representatives who are not part of the traditional purchasing relationship. Seek involvement of customer representatives from different functional areas. Ensure capable people interact with the customer team. A positive engagement which goes deeper into the customer organization increases the visibility of your company. Use quotations of customers and other external feedback to increase impact and soft power.

Soft power of consultation

Key executives in customer organizations impacted by a transformation were consulted during the planning phase. Most understood the rationale for change and participated enthusiastically, providing useful feedback. Two important customers expressed dissatisfaction with the plan, highlighting the importance of consultation and the requirement for closer engagement and regular feedback. Concerns were addressed as far as possible, communication lines remained open, and they were informed at every step. When the transformation completed successfully, concerns settled and the dissenting customers signed up to the new way of working.

Collaboration and support

Proactive offers of support and collaboration with colleagues and other departments generate favourable undertones and ensure reciprocal collaboration. Investing in collaboration fills a bucket of goodwill. The law of reciprocity as set out by Robert Cialdini in his book *Influence* describes the sense of obligation that builds from giving a gift or doing a favour, whether proactive or not. A natural feeling of indebtedness is forged when a person provides support or gives a gift even though nothing is required in return. The expectation created in the recipient is that a return favour of equal value is due, which often turns out be of greater value than the initial gift.[71]

Organizations are naturally organized into separate groups. Research shows how people in groups band together to rival another group.[72] If two friends are split into different groups which contain foes, in the event of rivalry, the common interest of their new group overrides the existing friendship. Evidence also suggests that putting groups together to achieve a common goal produces cooperative behaviour. Setting collaborative goals between two rival teams who need to work together to achieve the goal can change behaviour, improve performance, and form lasting relationships.

Strategic priority

The need for transformation may be connected to an existing critical business improvement strategy or a change in strategic direction. Where this is not immediately evident, overtly link the transformation outcome to the organization's strategic priorities. The more it is in tune with other plans, the more the programme garners support and investment, and the less likely it will be stopped prematurely. Build soft power by spelling out the connections when interacting with senior leaders.

---

[71] Robert Cialdini, *Influence: The Psychology of Persuasion*, HarperCollins, 2007, p. 17.
[72] Mark Leary, *Understanding the Mysteries of Human Behaviour*, The Teaching Company, 2012, p. 153.

Events and communications

Celebration events, progress updates, and milestone markers are important vehicles of soft power and indirect communication of culture. Attendance is largely voluntary; the audience is therefore receptive, providing the means for drip-feeding success stories, news, and benefits. Invest in preparation and cleverly presented graphics and videos for impact. Short, informative blogs and social media are sources of influence. Set up catchy news feeds. Celebrate success with stakeholders and collaborators. Bring fun to the process and create positive associations. Target stakeholders and relevant audiences with different emphasis; the more purpose designed the communication, the better the result.

People in authority

A healthy transformation programme enjoys broad sponsorship at senior levels within the organization. Engagement of senior team members brings legitimate power and helps influence contributors to play their part, sometimes through hard, but mostly soft, power. Senior sponsorship naturally exerts influence through holding teams to account for performance, prioritizing their focus, and highlighting the consequence of failure to engage and collaborate with the programme.

Diplomacy and exported talent

In politics, diplomacy is a core tool of soft power. A foreign ambassador represents their home country in important matters, and acts in support of unofficial matters which advocate for the home culture, ideology, and political interests. Diplomacy is also an effective soft power in organizations. Physically locate team members within other functional teams to pursue programme objectives and provide ambassadorship. Make sure these colleagues have the skills to influence. They are an important conduit between the programme team and other business teams, and a crucial medium through which connections can be made. Good leaders encourage cross-fertilization of talent in the organization. Team members who move into other areas of the business are potential ambassadors. Ensure people move in and out of the team in a positive way; discuss their informal diplomatic responsibility as they move. Offer continued connection and support for departing team members and secure their commitment to informal communication of common interests between the old and new team.

A unified team

A cohesive, unified, and loyal team perform better and exude confidence, increasing appeal and influence on other groups. When the team is easy to deal with, exciting to be with, supportive, and collaborative, positive values are transmitted. Unity is not easy to achieve at the best of times, and difficult times create tension and splinters. A disparate team with mixed loyalties damages the plan and reputation. We have discussed strategies for teams earlier in Chapter 5; however, to improve soft power, work relentlessly on team loyalty and inter-team relationships. Resolve conflicts and provide the team with tools and resources to face the rest of the organization confidently and competently. It is easier to recruit new people, collaborate, and gain sponsorship for a team with credibility and a great climate.

Training, education, and internal marketing

Providing information is a strategic endeavour. It is crucial to ensuring people have perspective, but it must not be fired off aimlessly. People are bombarded with messages daily and must therefore take on some and ignore others. When designed carefully to ensure its stickiness, timed appropriately, and targeted towards the right people at the right time, it is both respectful to the individual and likely to achieve the desired effect. Carefully pick times, moments, and venues to offer training and education for best results. Use a blend of approaches to support learning styles and agendas. Determine when personal contact or virtual solutions are appropriate. Process, discuss, and validate messaging to increase understanding, prevent misinterpretations, and test the extent to which it is driving real action and behaviour. Marketing is most effective when it meets a person's need at the right time. Stakeholder needs analysis and feedback provide insight into the appropriate marketing response.

Meetings

Meetings are manifestations of organization and team culture; they are prominent exhibitions of leadership style and values. Inefficient or bureaucratic meetings are wasteful and communicate mediocrity. Fast-paced, well-organized, accountable, and action-focused meetings communicate high performance. Consider the image and performance of the team at meetings. Agree protocols and a charter of behaviours. Use meetings to role model behaviours and practices. Find ways to reinforce aspects of the programme, team reputation, or any other messaging important to success. Ensure harmony and conflict; harmony is important for moving forward, whilst tension and conflict are required to surface problems.

Nudge principles

Nudging is a behavioural science concept which proposes engineering of choices offering positive reinforcement and indirect suggestions to influence the behaviour and decision making of groups and individuals. Richard Thaler and Cass Sunstein, in their book *Nudge*, give the following definition of a nudge: 'any aspect of the choice architecture that alters people's behaviour in a predictable way without forbidding any options or significantly changing their economic incentives'. Three principles guide the use of nudges:[73]

1. All nudges should be transparent and never misleading.
2. It should be as easy as possible to opt out of the nudge.
3. There should be good reason to believe that the behaviour being encouraged will improve the welfare of those being nudged.

As an example, assisted self-service check-in kiosks were offered alongside traditional check-in with the aim of nudging travellers towards owning production of the boarding pass. Once accustomed to the process, travellers were quick to convert to online options and kiosks were replaced.

Set up choices. Encourage or nudge people towards the option with the best impact on their welfare, whilst allowing for opt out or alternative choices. Nudge principles can be used for aspects of employee engagement, welfare, or customer engagement, and for helping people adjust to new ways of working. Automatic enrolment to a training course with an ability to cancel or select a different medium or date would constitute a nudge.

Conclusion

There we have it. In this game of winning hearts and minds, smart power is the answer. The conscious awareness of power and influence, the distinction between selective hard power and, more often, soft power, builds confidence, credibility, and support for the transformation over the long term. On that note we will explore the final power, also important for sustainability: staying power.

---

[73] Richard Thaler and Cass Sunstein, *Nudge: Improving Decisions about Health, Wealth and Happiness*, Penguin, 2009, p. 6.

Action points

1. Use soft power to build influence, change culture, and sustain transformation. Start work in the visioning phase or earlier.
2. Know how aspects of structure, organization of work, and process contribute to power within the organization. Factor this into planning for transformation and the design of organization, process, work sharing, and accountability.
3. Use hard power selectively and employ a range of soft power strategies to influence widely and subtly within the organization.

Chapter 8

Staying power

Introduction

When organizations launch a major transformation effort, experts warn of the many ambitious plans which fail to live up to expectations. The dispiriting failure rate quoted is around 75%. It's true that the forces which manifest to derail a programme are infinite: a gap in capability causing the loss of customers or confidence in the plan; a major overspend or technology problems; leadership resistance and lack of vision; culture and failure to adapt in line with the new plan; financial challenges like a shortage of resources or economic downturn. And the list goes on. This book has been concerned with preventing such failures by taking care of the people stuff.

McKinsey & Company surveyed leaders and reported the actions more frequently associated with successful transformation.[74] If the senior management team communicated openly and across the organization about transformation progress and results, a successful outcome was eight times more likely. If leaders role modelled the behaviours required from the change, success was 5.3 times more likely. It was 3.9 times more likely if senior managers were held accountable for their contribution to transformation, and 5.5 times more likely if everyone understood how their work relates to the organization's vision. We have explored how these very factors can be assured when you transform by activating personal power, and in doing so transform the world around you with goal, process, people, culture, and smart power. There

---

[74] Dana Maor, Angelika Reich, and Lara Yocarini, *The People Power of Transformations*, McKinsey & Company, 2017.

is, however, one more important power, a side effect of activating other powers. Staying power is the organizational and leadership resilience required to navigate difficulties and convert obstacles into opportunities.

We will now consider the resilience factors important to transformation. These factors have arisen during the preceding chapters; however, here we emphasize their importance for building staying power and seeing through ambitious plans.

A recipe for resilience

The ten ingredients inherent in the six powers, which create staying power are: culture, character, continuity, competence, confidence, connection, contribution, control, customer, and conditions.

Culture

As we saw in Chapter 6, a high-performing culture is characterized by leaders with the right style and character, who embrace people, and maintain accountability, customer intimacy, and excellence. Furthermore, it is the protective shield which deflects potential derailers. The continual development of people and leaders builds flexibility and confidence to deal with adversity. The policies and practices of compassion build psychological safety, whilst open dialogue surfaces issues early. Constructive accountability ensures quick decision making and action. Customer intimacy maintains external focus and innovation. Excellence retains employees and customers. We saw in Chapter 4 the importance of identifying cultural strengths and placing them at the heart of the change to ensure success.

Fixing the heart

A business transforming back-office services and processes experienced a serious dip in morale with widespread resistance. The executive team paused the plan and engaged a third party to survey leadership and employee opinion. Whilst some resistance was typical, results revealed a deep concern for the impact of internal changes on customer relationships. The top team decided to redesign the programme. Customer experience was positioned front and centre. Enhancing customer value became the core aim of every new process and proposed changes which did not meet these criteria could not progress. Customer representatives were enlisted to work streams and consulted as advisers; their feedback was processed, validated, and incorporated into design and implementation. The new approach resulted in employee and customer engagement spikes. Customer focus was so strong within the company that the transformation, as originally conceived, seemed alien. The use of this cultural strength in relaunch created new purpose, allayed fears, and put teams back in the driving seat.

Character

Character implies courage, a survivor's wisdom, conviction for what's right, and a preparedness to sacrifice and do the right thing. A leadership with character creates curiosity, followership, and citizenship in others through their guiding values and integrity. Such leaders role model equality and democracy, a place where members embrace opinions and conflicts, and debate and resolve issues. They give people a reason to fight for what they believe in, the strength to defend a position, to stand up for others, and to do what they think is right. Transformation is carried through by the will and commitment of people in the organization who respond best to a consistent, driven leadership with conviction and passion for their cause.

Continuity

Some organizations change leaders like they are going out of fashion. Change provides career progression and prevents stagnation, but it can be stressful for the team who need to build new rapport and demonstrate their contribution to a new boss. New leaders inevitably want to make their mark by overhauling practices and habits to modernize or improve efficiency. Continuity of leader and team enables change programmes and initiatives to be completed efficiently. Begin transformation with an established leader and team. Ideally, relationships have been developed with new project team recruits or experts ahead of time. Leaders with tenure and history can more easily reposition existing initiatives to fit the new context. If earlier work is disregarded and disrespected, employees lose faith in every new initiative launched.

Competence

An organization with deep capabilities and openness to new learning is resilient, confident in their plan, able to anticipate issues and draw on wide experience for quick decision making and maintains service to customers during change. The competence to transform includes the ability of the team and the wider organization to deliver the programme, and the thinking agility to handle unexpected issues. A transformation team and collaborators who demonstrate calm competence reassure the organization and deflect resistance.

Competence breeds confidence

In one organization, sceptical business leaders required a checkpoint at which the transformation would stop if expectations hadn't been met. At the first checkpoint the programme exceeded the target and implementation was smooth. The competence of the team installing the processes, managing the transition, deploying technology, and training other staff proved so strong that the next phase was approved instantly. It too demonstrated effective planning, cautious implementation timings, well-managed risks, and seamless deployment. Dissent fizzled out and the programme accelerated. The checkpoints became milestone celebrations.

Confidence

Thriving in change requires a feeling of confidence, the mental strength to keep going. Confidence is a consequence of competence and earlier successful experience. It is also derived from conviction in the plan, an unshakeable knowledge that it is the right solution. Confidence can be easily knocked when faults or disruption occur. Whilst a problem may imply a need for review, it is not a reason to lose confidence. A loss of confidence by project owners infects the team, the wider organization, and investors. A leader must respond with analysis rather than emotion and deploy a confident style to reassure the team. Revisit the text on symbiotic teams in Chapter 5 for information on confident leadership.

Connection

No man (or person) is an island; we can only achieve our goals with the support of others and the power of community. Connections become crucial when a project hits roadblocks. Use relationships and dynamically networked connections to provide skills, ideas, influence, or emotional support when necessary. Organize or structure for collaboration. Foster connections with stakeholders to ensure relationships are strong enough to withstand conflict and sustain through challenging times. A communication and involvement strategy keeps stakeholders engaged and increases support in difficult times.

Contribution

The human need to feel significant and valued is a powerful source of energy; it pushes people to act, and seek achievement and fulfilment. This motivational force contributes to change momentum if harnessed yet is easily ignored in a busy environment. Feed this need by ensuring contribution is clarified, reinforced, and celebrated. It energizes and revives a change-weary team. Change can destroy existing purpose and appear to devastate the results of years of work and effort. Recognize previous contribution, link it to the new way of working, and offer purpose in the new world to motivate the team. See Chapter 5.

Control

Psychological studies prove that freedom of choice and action positively impact performance, mental wellbeing, and resilience. This feeling of control over our destiny is central to happiness. Change imposed on a group of people disrupts a well-ordered way of life, so restoring a sense of control is vital. People must relinquish some control in the interest of progress; it's important to replace this with something they can control. Take time to understand the way in which control is removed from the team and determine how you can put them back in charge of their destiny.

Regaining control

For a team of international professionals, the arrival of a plan to increase efficiency appeared removed from the real world of their country and operating team. Early communication led to fear of lost power and control. A continuous flow of communication, education, and consultation raised awareness and sought buy-in; however, the team continued to resist emotionally. Mental health training helped the team to analyse and disassociate from their reactions and behaviours and recognize the personal impact of resisting the inevitable. After training, objectivity improved, mindsets adjusted, and the group took ownership of implementation and for making the change fit their own teams. Many assumed programme-wide responsibilities which increased their ability to see the bigger picture and influence key decisions.

Customer

A business obsessed with customer value and putting the customer first weathers change better. Relationships are strong and loyalty is more likely to sustain during difficult times. The customer focus provides a golden thread that maintains employee attention and purpose during uncertainty. See 'Customer culture' in Chapter 6.

Conditions

We have evolved to be alert to the dangers of change, so it is instinctively threatening until we are able to prove to ourselves otherwise. Just knowing that this feeling is normal is helpful to mental health. Personal power provides confidence and self-awareness that help us bounce back. When we operate from inner values, a clear purpose, and conviction, it's difficult to knock confidence. We can observe our emotional response, stop, reflect, analyse the feelings, and respond rationally. We more readily recognize the potential of change to create good things. When this happens, we become resourceful and able to fight our way through the challenges. To build resilience in the team, concentrate on providing the conditions and tools that help.

Conclusion

A willingness to stay open to alternative ideas or options. A penchant for innovation and learning. The decisiveness and agility to adjust plans, practices, and resources to meet changing circumstances, yet keeping true to the vision. These characteristics amount to the ability to return and learn from life-threatening situations, capitalize on challenges, and reinvent when necessary. They ensure the team can stay the course of an ambitious transformation and achieve the ultimate outperformance.

Action points

1. Use the ten resilience factors to evaluate change readiness. Identify gaps and act to ensure the team and organization can stay the course.
2. Train and familiarize others with the mental strategies for personal resilience, mental strength, self-compassion, managing emotions, mindfulness, and stress management. See Chapter 2.
3. Use psychometrics and other tools for increasing self-awareness, discussed in Chapter 2.
4. Educate in the transformational power of the S curve and develop understanding of change and reactions to change. See Chapters 1 and 4.

5. Reinvigorate the team purpose and help individuals to find and align their purpose. See Chapters 2 and 5.
6. Encourage positive relationships through team building and other interventions. See Chapter 5.
7. Set up caring committees of buddy, mentor, coach, friend, and counsellor relationships.

Outperformance

This book is concerned with bringing about the conditions for the outperformance of a leader, their team, and organization. We outperform when we exceed current expectations or the performance of our peers and industry competitors, when we sustain the performance differential over time in a range of circumstances, and when we become distinct. To outperform we must know our comparators, their current and historic performance, and circumstances. Are their results reliable? Are they consistent? What circumstances worked for and against them? What skills and talents do they possess and how do they use them? What contextual factors help or hinder them? A sporting team must understand the performance of competitor teams over sustained sporting seasons. Business teams study industry performance and how competitors do what they do; what talent they have and how they shape up against industry metrics or ratios. Individuals competing against a peer or their own expectations must understand their own best and current performance and that of their comparator. A performance which is 25% better than last year is irrelevant unless performing against a shallower uplift in the competitor's performance.

Organizations, teams, or individuals can derive inspiration from others; however, a vision of what, and a plan of how, to deliver the difference that makes the difference is imperative. Performance must be at least one step beyond the competitor's, improve productivity a degree more, achieve results a level higher, and develop distinct mastery. As soon as the target performance is in line of sight, reinvention and innovation must initiate a new, steeper performance curve. This is what it takes to outperform and doing so requires unbreakable faith in our ability to achieve a mission;

it requires a culture of discipline, a continuous desire to win, an amazing support system of people who care, and the capacity to refuel energy levels during the most challenging times.

Leader

Outperformance requires a lifetime of reinvention, a personal transformation of the leader interwoven with that of the team, in a double helix of performance peaks, learning troughs, and transformation moments. As we have seen, it means maximizing personal power, goal power, process power, people power, culture power, smart power, and staying power, which fuse to manifest superpower at critical times: the moment when extraordinary talent meets extraordinary challenge and something magic happens. The revelation of performance so special it reverberates widely and impacts others in many wonderful ways. As we discovered in Chapter 2, the first step is getting connected with the person behind the performance, the person behind the leader. The personality, with all its quirks, talents, and imperfections, when freed and nurtured can grow to great heights. Who are you as a leader? What emotions drive or distract you? What do you want to do with your life? What are you passionate about? Who do you want to serve and affect? What are your values and how do you reinforce them through your actions? High performers understand their strengths, values, and vulnerabilities, and act from this insight. This congruence becomes the force which delivers and the basis of a consistent, recognizable brand identity, which compounds and strengthens impact.

The super leader and their team transform and reinvent routinely. Each time they do, they grow stronger through experience and learning, which they translate into new performance. Whilst they develop and change internally, their brand remains consistent and strong. Their principles and self-assurance enable a vision and conviction so strong they can't be diverted from the goal. They form a single-minded view of the world and their future in it, and they move unapologetically towards it. With every obstacle they collect new insight for future use. Their style, even if unconventional, motivates and inspires and they know how to make this work for them. Their principles and opinions are so coherent they magnify and attract others. This ability to remain grounded and connected to their primal inclinations, whilst focused on the future vision, ensures they never stay still and are only passing through to something higher.

Every superhero needs to know when they fit and when to split, which of course means starting the next S curve. Every leader has a context which best suits their personality and one which suits it least. They can only continue to outperform if, at times, they recognize the need to move on, often when it hurts the most; a time when they have delivered repeated outperformance but before the context changes, forcing a dip in performance. A great leader has developed and grown their team to the point that, at a given moment, their best choice is to pass the baton to a worthy successor who will hopefully take the team to new heights.

Team

Strong teams are small and beautiful. Teams consist of individuals with their own personal power and talent which must be released, deployed, and enabled through a capable leader. The leader understands how to wield the SABRE of personal power, and IMPACT to unleash superpower, as we saw in Chapter 2. They can EMBRACE SELF, develop a brand, fascinate, inspire others to a glorious vision, coach and develop the team, and engage them with a CIRCLE OF TRUST. They create SPACE, a culture containing the nutritious soil in which the team can grow beyond the initial expectations they set for themselves. The image of an outperforming team is one that wins consistently, whose talents come together in the moment to provide the solution for their game. They become SYMBIOTIC resulting from bonded relationships, pursuit of excellence, improving every aspect of their performance, and practising continuously. They show concern for the team over the individual and are content to let one person shine in the interests of team success for which they are acclaimed and rewarded. Whilst there may be stars amongst the team, every member has a valuable and specific talent without which the team would not perform to their best and the stars would not shine. They have the tools to manage their emotions to maximize the psychology of performance, enabled through the coaching of the leader and their caring committee.

Organization

Successful organizations contain many teams whose efforts and outcomes converge to deliver greatness. The executive leadership understand the importance of the team. They focus on developing talented teams in the belief that this will breed individual top talent. They also provide the team with the resources and freedom to explode their potential, reaping the results of long-term performance. Great companies have a culture of discipline, avoiding bureaucracy and the temptation to create universal rules to deal with a small group of non-conformers. Instead, they provide a rigorous framework with clear freedoms, ensure people are accountable, and follow through to the level of detail and persistence that ensures the job is done well. Such companies are clear about what they can become the best in the world at. They know when to do things differently, even if it means reinventing their operating model. These organizations are clear about their mission and the economics that best demonstrate their performance. The top leader displays extraordinary drive to achieve success for the organization and build the company for the long term. They are low profile, humble, modest, and determined, often grown inside the company, uncompromising in choosing people and developing leaders.

Whether you are interested in your own performance, are a leader of a small team in search of better results, or charged with the hefty task of transforming a large organization, the characteristics of outperformance and interventions shared throughout this book should help. These ideas and approaches have been developed and gathered through my own experience and are neither finite nor indisputable. I only hope that you find food for thought and something that enhances your approach. I wish you every success in your endeavours to transform and outperform and am thankful for the opportunity to share my thoughts with you. I would love to hear from you if you would like to share any reflections or, indeed, if you need help implementing any recommendations in this book, please contact me at transform2outperform.com.

Bibliography

Chapter 1

Bezos, Jeff, CNBC interview. 1999. Available from https://m. youtube.com/watch?v=GltlJO56S1g [accessed 19 May 2022].

Carlin, John. 2008. *Playing the Enemy: Nelson Mandela and the Game That Made a Nation*. Atlantic Books.

Christensen, Clayton M. 2016. *The Innovator's Dilemma*. Harvard Business Review Press.

Christensen, Clayton M., Raynor, Michael E., and McDonald, R. 2015. 'What is disruptive innovation?' *Harvard Business Review*, December 2015. Available from https://hbr.org/2015/12/what-is-disruptive-innovation [accessed 19 May 2022].

Collins, Jim. 2001. *Good to Great: Why Some Companies Make the Leap and Others Don't*. Random House Business Books.

Handy, Charles. 2016. *The Second Curve*. Penguin Random House.

Holbeche, Linda. 2015. *The Agile Organization: How to Build an Engaged, Innovative and Resilient Business*. Kogan Page.

Mandela, Nelson. 1994. *Long Walk to Freedom*. Little Brown.

Obama, Michelle. 2018. *Becoming*. Penguin Random House.

Peppler, Lance. 2019. 'The amazing Flywheel Effect – succeed like Amazon'. *The Business Bookshelf*, 18 October 2019. Available from www.businessbookshelfpodcast.com/post/the-amazing-flywheel-effect-succeed-like-amazon [accessed 19 May 2022].

Chapter 2

Alberts, Hugo. 2018. 'A coaching masterclass on meaning and valued living'. Positive Psychology Program BV.

Ericsson, K. Anders, Krampe, Ralf T., and Tesch-Römer, Clemens. 1993. 'The role of deliberate practice in the acquisition of expert performance'. *Psychological Review*, 100(3): 363. https://psycnet.apa.org/buy/1993-40718-001

Eurich, Tascha. 2018. 'What self-awareness really is (and how to cultivate it)' (HBR Emotional Intelligence Series). *Harvard Business Review*, 4 January 2018. Available from https://hbr.org/2018/01/what-self-awareness-really-is-and-how-to-cultivate-it [accessed 19 May 2022].

Frankl, Victor E. 2004 (1959). *Man's Search for Meaning*. Random House.

Greene, Robert. 2012. *Mastery*. Profile Books Ltd.

Hogshead, Sally. 2014. *How the World Sees You: Discover Your Highest Value Through the Science of Fascination*. HarperCollins.

Hogshead, Sally. 2016. *Fascinate: Your 7 Triggers to Persuasion and Captivation: Unlocking the Secret Triggers of Influence, Persuasion, and Captivation*. HarperCollins.

Ibarra, Herminia and Lineback, Kent. 2005. 'What's your story?', *Harvard Business Review*, January 2005. Available from https://hbr.org/2005/01/whats-your-story [accessed 19 May 2022].

Jensen, Mark P., Adachi, Tomonori, and Hakimian, Shahin. 2015. 'Brain oscillations, hypnosis, and hypnotizability'. *The American*

Journal of Clinical Hypnosis, 57(3): 230–253. Available from www.ncbi.nlm.nih.gov/pmc/articles/PMC4361031/ [accessed 19 May 2022].

Kaplan, Robert E. and Kaiser, Robert B. 2009. 'Stop overdoing your strengths'. *Harvard Business Review*, February 2009. Available from https://hbr.org/2009/02/stop-overdoing-your-strengths [accessed 19 May 2022].

Leary, Mark. 2018. *Why You Are Who You Are: Investigations into Human Personality*. The Great Courses.

Mayer, John, D. 2014. 'Know thyself'. *Psychology Today*, 11 March 2014. Available from www.psychologytoday.com/us/articles/201403/know-thyself [accessed 19 May 2022].

Morgan Roberts, Laura, Spreitzer, Gretchen M., Dutton, Jane E., Quinn, Robert E., Heaphy, Emily, and Barker, Brianna. 2005. 'How to play to your strengths'. *Harvard Business Review*, January 2005. Available from https://hbr.org/2005/01/how-to-play-to-your-strengths [accessed 19 May 2022].

Pattakos, Alex. 2010. *Prisoners of Our Thoughts*. Berrett-Koehler Inc.

Quinn, Robert E. 2005. 'Moments of greatness: Entering the fundamental state of leadership'. *Harvard Business Review*, July–August 2005. Available from https://hbr.org/2005/07/moments-of-greatness-entering-the-fundamental-state-of-leadership [accessed 19 May 2022].

Silvester, Trevor. 2010. *Cognitive Hypnotherapy: What's That About and How Can I Use It?* Matador/Troubador Publishing Ltd.

Wolinsky, Stephen. 1991. *Trances People Live: Healing Approaches in Quantum Psychology*. Bramble Books.

Chapter 3

Adams, A.J. 2009. 'Seeing is believing: The power of visualization'. *Psychology Today*, 3 December 2009. Available from www.psychologytoday.com/gb/blog/flourish/200912/seeing-is-believing-the-power-visualization [accessed 19 May 2022].

Harvard Business Review on Change. 1998. Harvard Business School Press.

Heath, Chip and Heath, Dan. 2008. *Made to Stick: Why Some Ideas Survive and Others Die*. Arrow.

Kotler, Steven. 2014. *The Rise of Superman: Decoding the Science of Ultimate Human Performance*. Quercus Editions Ltd.

Steinmann, Barbara, Klug, Hannah P., and Maier, Günter W. 2018. 'The path is the goal: How transformational leaders enhance followers' job attitudes and proactive behavior'. *Frontiers in Psychology*, 9: 2338. https://doi.org/10.3389/fpsyg.2018.02338

Chapter 4

Cable, Daniel M. 2018. *Alive at Work: The Neuroscience of Helping Your People Love What They Do*. Harvard Business Review Press.

Dewar, Carolyn and Keller, Scott. 2009. 'The irrational side of change management'. McKinsey & Company, 1 April 2009. Available from www.mckinsey.com/business-functions/people-and-organizational-performance/our-insights/the-irrational-side-of-change-management [accessed 19 May 2022].

Dilts, Robert. 2003. *From Coach to Awakener*. Dilts Strategy Group.

Gazzaley, Adam and Rozen, Larry D. 2016. *The Distracted Mind: Ancient Brains in a High-Tech World*. MIT Press.

Keller, Scott and Schaninger, Bill. 2019. 'A better way to lead large-scale change'. McKinsey & Company, July 2019.

Keller, Scott and Schaninger, Bill. 2019. 'Getting personal about change'. McKinsey & Company, August 2019.

Kotter, John. 2012. *Leading Change: An Action Plan from the World's Foremost Expert on Business Leadership*. Harvard Business Review Press.

Panksepp, Jaak, 2010. 'Affective neuroscience of the emotional BrainMind: Evolutionary perspectives and implications for understanding depression'. *Dialogues in Clinical Neuroscience*, 12(4): 533–545. https://doi.org/10.31887/DCNS.2010.12.4/jpanksepp

Whitmore, John. 2009. *Coaching for Performance: The Principles and Practice of Coaching and Leadership*. Nicholas Brealey Publishing, 2009.

Chapter 5

Amabile, Teresa and Kramer, Steven. 2011. *The Progress Principle: Using Small Wins to Ignite Joy, Engagement, and Creativity at Work*. Harvard Business Review Press.

Amabile, Teresa M. 2012. 'Componential theory of creativity', April 2012. Available from www.hbs.edu/ris/Publication%20Files/12-096.pdf [accessed 19 May 2022].

Amabile, Teresa M., Barsade, Sigal G., Mueller, Jennifer S., and Staw, Barry M. 2005. 'Affect and creativity at work'. *Administrative Science Quarterly*, 50: 367–403. https://doi.org/10.2189%2Fasqu.2005.50.3.367

Bjork, Robert R.A. and Bjork, Elizabeth L. 2020. 'Desirable difficulties in theory and practice'. *Journal of Applied Research in Memory and Cognition*, 9(4): 475–479. https://doi.org/10.1016/j.jarmac.2020.09.003

Csikszentmihalyi, Mihaly. 2002. *Flow: The Psychology of Optimal Experience*. Rider.

Cuddy, Amy. 2015. *Presence: Bringing Your Boldest Self to Your Biggest Challenge*. Little, Brown and Company.

Cuddy, Amy J.C., Wilmuth, Caroline A., and Carney, Dana. 2012. 'The benefit of power posing before a high-stakes social evaluation'. Harvard Business School Working Paper, No 013-027, September 2012. Available from http://nrs.harvard.edu/urn-3:HUL.Inst Repos:9547823 [accessed 19 May 2022].

Darwin, Charles R. 2009. *The Descent of Man, and Selection in Relation to Sex*. Digireads.com.

Fabritius, Friederike and Hagemann, Hans W. 2018. *The Leading Brain: Neuroscience Hacks to Work Smarter, Better, Happier*. TarcherPerigee.

Fletcher, Louise cited in 'Jack Nicholson at 80: Life in pictures'. *BBC Arts*. Available from. www.bbc.co.uk/programmes/articles/58DD9bbxm2rfPfFSLd1TZ&p/jack-nicholson-at-80-life-in-pictures [accessed 19 May 2022].

Fraser, Alice. 2020. 'All being well: A brief history of wellness'. Audible podcast.

Henriques, Martha. 2019. 'Can the legacy of trauma be passed down the generations?' *BBC*, 26 March 2019. Available from www. bbc.com/future/article/20190326-what-is-epigenetics [accessed 19 May 2022].

Jack Nicholson scene preparation. Available from https://youtu.be/ Qu3xxq5F3Gw [accessed 19 May 2022].

Jamieson, Jeremy P. et al. 2012. 'Mind over matter: Reappraising arousal improves cardiovascular and cognitive responses to stress'. *Journal of Experimental Psychology*, 141(3): 417–422.

Keller, Abiola et al. 2012. 'Does the perception that stress affects health matter? The association with health and mortality'. *Health Psychology*, 31(5): 677–684.

Kolb, David A. 1984. *Experiential Learning: Experience as the Source of Learning and Development*. Prentice Hall.

Lipton, Bruce. 2015. *The Biology of Belief: Unleashing the Power of Consciousness, Matter & Miracles*. Hay House UK.

McGonigal, Kelly. 'How to make stress your friend', TEDGlobal 2013, June 2013. Available from www.ted.com/talks/kelly_ mcgonigal_how_to_make_stress_your_friend [accessed 19 May 2022].

Patterson, Kerry, Grenny, Joseph, McMillan, Ron, and Switzler, Al. 2011. *Crucial Conversations: Tools for Talking When Stakes Are High*. McGraw Hill.

Poulin, Michael J., Brown, Stephanie L., Dillard, Amanda J., and Smith, Dylan M. 2013. 'Giving to others and the association between stress and mortality'. *American Journal of Public Health*, 103(9): 1649–1655.

Rizzolatti, Giacomo and Sinigaglia, Corrado. 2008. *Mirrors in the Brain: How Our Minds Share Actions and Emotions*. Oxford University Press.

Vance, Erik. 2016. *Suggestible You: The Curious Science of Your Brain's Ability to Deceive, Transform and Heal*. National Geographic Partners.

Chapter 6

Atif, M. 2019. 'Reinventing personalization for customer experience: Why? What? How?' Towards Data Science, 30 May 2019. Available from https://towardsdatascience.com/reinventing-personalization-for-customer-experience-235d8c75aa38 [accessed 19 May 2022].

Cialdini, Robert. 2007. *Influence: The Psychology of Persuasion*. HarperCollins.

Connors, Roger and Smith, Tom. 2012. *Change the Culture, Change the Game: The Breakthrough Strategy for Energizing Your Organization and Creating Accountability for Results*. Portfolio.

Dive, Brian. 2008. *The Accountable Leader: Developing Effective Leadership, Through Managerial Accountability*. Kogan Page.

Finneman, Bo, Ivory, Julia, Marchessou, Sophie, Schmidt, Jennifer, and Skiles, Tom. 2017. 'Cracking the code on millennial consumers'. McKinsey & Company, 18 March 2017. Available from www.mckinsey.com/industries/retail/our-insights/cracking-the-code-on-millennial-consumers [accessed 19 May 2022].

Goleman, Daniel. 2000. 'Leadership that gets results'. *Harvard Business Review*, March–April 2000.

Great Place to Work. 2019. 'Fortune 100 Best Companies to Work For® 2019'. Available from www.greatplacetowork.com/best-workplaces/100-best/2019 [accessed 19 May 2022].

Heath, Chip and Heath, Dan. 2017. *The Power of Moments: Why Certain Experiences Have Extraordinary Impact.* Penguin Random House.

Pine, Joseph II and Gilmore, James H. 1998. 'Welcome to the experience economy'. *Harvard Business Review*, July–August 1998.

Porath, Christine. 2014. 'Half of employees don't feel respected by their bosses'. *Harvard Business Review*, 19 November 2014. Available from https://hbr.org/2014/11/half-of-employees-dont-feel-respected-by-their-bosses [accessed 19 May 2022].

Spearhead Training, 'Leadership and engagement'. Available from www.spearhead-training.co.uk/blog/leadership-and-engagement [accessed 19 May 2022].

Stone, Dorian and Maynes, Joel. 2014. 'For customer loyalty, only the best will do'. McKinsey & Company, 1 February 2014. Available from www.mckinsey.com/business-functions/growth-marketing-and-sales/our-insights/for-customer-loyalty-only-the-best-will-do [accessed 19 May 2022].

Chapter 7

Leary, Mark. 2012. *Understanding the Mysteries of Human Behaviour*. The Teaching Company.

Nye, Joseph S. 2004. *Soft Power: The Means to Success in World Politics*. Public Affairs.

Nye, Joseph S. 2008. *The Powers to Lead*. Oxford University Press.

Thaler, Richard and Sunstein, Cass. 2009. *Nudge: Improving Decisions about Health, Wealth and Happiness*. Penguin.

Chapter 8

Maor, Dana, Reich, Angelika, and Yocarini, Lara. 2017. *The People Power of Transformations*. McKinsey & Company.

Index

Note: Page numbers in **bold** indicate tables; those in *italics* indicate figures.